LETTERS TO WILLIAM

First published in 2022 by
New Life Publishing, Luton,
Bedfordshire LU3 4DQ

© Margaret Stevens

British Library Cataloguing in Publication Data
A catalogue record for this book is available
from the British Library

ISBN 978 1 912237 39 5

Typesetting by New Life Publishing,
Luton, UK www.goodnewsbooks.co.uk
Printed and bound in Great Britain

LETTERS TO WILLIAM

A witness to the One, Holy,
Catholic and Apostolic Faith

MARGARET STEVENS

I dedicate this book to

The Holy Family of Nazareth

CONTENTS

FOREWORD

'The whole concern of doctrine and its teaching
must be directed to the love that never ends.'
Catechism of the Catholic Church (CCC) 251

Dear Reader,

My name is William. The letters you are about to read were
written to me when I was still a young man and wanted to find
out what being a Christian might mean. I was put in touch with
a distant relative, the only Catholic in our family, 'Auntie May'.

You see, I was confused at the time by what I had so far learned
from two sources. My college teachers and my fellow students
were giving me a general Protestant view, from rather different
standpoints, but agreeing in not having much time for Catholics.

We corresponded over a period of some three years, and I felt
all along that my questions were well answered. It was only later
that I realised how I had been led to a personal knowledge of
our loving God, in the fullness of the Church that Jesus gave to
his Apostles. Because of the JOY I found, I have decided to share
with you what was written to me during this, the first stage of
what I can only call my 'adventure with God.'

PART ONE

TO A YOUNG MAN

FIRST LETTER

Dear William,

I was delighted to hear from you and to learn that you are exploring what it means to be a true Christian!

You say your fellow students have led you to various Christian fellowships and worship groups, but you find it confusing. There are so many. They all claim to have the right answers. You wonder why they do not all join together.

You have bought a Bible. Excellent!

You also say your History course has led you to explore the differences between Protestants and Catholics, and some of your new friends have no time for Catholics. And, again, you wonder why. You would like to know the truth, and that is why you decided to track me down – the only Catholic in our huge family – and find out what I have to say.

I have not always been a Catholic, you know. That means I can share my knowledge of the Catholic Faith as someone who has been led to it. Add to that many years of living it and I think (I hope) you have come to the right person.

3

So where do we start? As you and I have not met while you were growing up, first we need to say something more about ourselves. Then I shall know, as they say, 'where you are coming from' and be better able to answer.

About me. Well, I am a second cousin to your grandmother, though born some years later, and have always been known to the younger generation as 'Auntie May'. You have my address. Yes, I bought this cottage after I was widowed and live alone with my dog, Cuthbert.

Now, what else? When I was much younger, I was two other kinds of Christian before becoming a Catholic, or 'coming into the Church' as we Catholics say. And I have recently done a Catholic course of study to add to my experience.

You tell me that you had your twentieth birthday not long ago, and are living away from home, and studying. It's a wonderful time of life, and I do hope you are enjoying it.

Can you tell me more about when you were very young; when you were still at home with both parents? I seem to remember seeing photos of your Christening. Was that in the village church? Does this mean you were brought up as a churchgoer?

You see, apart from anything else, we need to understand the way each of us uses certain words (like 'church' for instance) that are common to all Christians but for Catholics may have a particular meaning.

I'll stop there, but please do write again, because I'd love to hear more. Tell me about the History stuff, please. As well as about things to do with what you have so far found out about Christianity today. I'll do my best to give you sound and helpful answers.

I'll be looking forward to hearing from you!

By the way, you said you bought a Bible. Which one? And did you really not have one before?

God bless and keep you!

Your friend,
Auntie May

SECOND LETTER

Dear William,

So glad you liked my letter.

I enjoyed your description of yourself as a little boy going to church at Christmas and loving the crib and the carol singing. But was that all you knew? Did no-one teach you about God at all? Your parents? Your school?

I am sincere in asking and have more than one reason for it. One is that we need to prepare the ground before I start on what Catholics believe. I'm talking here of how and why our teaching differs from that of others who set out to be followers of Jesus.

I have so many questions! You gave the impression that your interest is not just to do with your studies, and you are definitely seeking a personal relationship with Jesus Christ who, as your friends will tell you, is indeed our Lord and Saviour. We all agree there.

Now, bear with me while I ask about your Good News Bible. I rather thought that would be the one. How do you find it? Above all, does it convince you that God loves you? After all, this is what the Bible is all about. Its basic teaching is quite simply this: God created us and loves us and wants each one of us to have a personal relationship with him. I should say here that Catholics often refer to the Bible as 'sacred Scripture' or simply 'Scripture'.

Because this amazing love of God is what the whole of Scripture is about, I'm simply dying to share with you certain verses. I'll put them at the end of my letter, hoping you'll find them helpful.

We haven't got started on the questions arising out of your studies, have we? So what exactly are your history specialists telling you about the 'Reformation' when Protestants arose and began to criticise the Catholic Church? Be prepared. I bet I'll soon be telling you what those specialists are not telling you!

I do hope you will get back to me soon.

'SCRIPTURES'
Try reading straight through the Book of Genesis Chapters 1 and 2. These verses establish that all life is a gift of God, he is the Creator, and we are the crown of God's creation, made in his image.[1]

Maybe put Chapter 3 on 'Hold' for the time being. Not that it's unimportant. Far from it. What happened there made a massive difference to humanity, and what all Christians call 'salvation' (being saved) became necessary to deliver us from its effects.

---

[1] Genesis 1:27

It is the reason why God kept sending his messengers (prophets) in the Old Testament part of the Bible, and, finally, sent his Son, Jesus Christ.[2] More of this as we go on!

For now, why not skip straight to the Christian part of the Bible, the New Testament, and to John's Gospel, Chapter 1, and read to the end of verse 14. Decide what you make of that. Then go straight to the beginning of the First Letter of John and read to the end of verse 3. The same message of LOVE is in all these.

By the way, you do know, don't you, that Jesus told his disciples: 'I am the Way: I am Truth and Life'?[3] You'll find I come back to that many times as well as to John's GOD IS LOVE.

That will have to do for now. I'm so glad we've agreed to stay in touch. Really! I can't wait to hear from you again.

Your friend,
Auntie May

---

[2] Hebrews 1: 1-3
[3] John 14:26

THIRD LETTER

Field Cottage,
6th Sunday of Easter

Dear William,

So good to hear from you. The first thing you will notice is that I have wiped the dust off my trusty old typewriter and am using that instead of confronting you with my handwriting, which suffers a bit from arthritis these days. Typing is easier.

History. I am not surprised that the Catholics come across as the 'baddies'. Our history books reflect the strong Protestant bias in our part of the world. After all, here in England, when Henry VIII – for personal reasons to do with marriage – declared himself Head of the Church in our country, it first became 'wrong' and then became 'dangerous' to claim that the Pope was still the true Head. That's how Henry came to put to death as 'traitors' his own chancellor, Thomas More, and Bishop John Fisher.[1]

In the reigns that followed (except for Mary's), gradual changes were made to the way worship was conducted in what we now know as the Church of England and everyone had to attend the services of this new Church. The changes made to the Church of England service known as 'Holy Communion' are significant.

---

[1] These two English martyrs are remembered on June 22nd

It gradually became very different from the Catholic Mass, which is in essence the same today as it always was.

Any in this country who still wanted to belong (as all had done before) to the One Holy Catholic and Apostolic Church, of which the Pope was the Head, were in trouble!! Priests from abroad were smuggled in to say Mass in secret and everyone involved came under persecution. Ask yourself, though, why so many were prepared to be put to death (in a terrible way!) rather than agree to deny their Catholic beliefs. We still sing about those times in a hymn called, 'Faith of our Fathers'.

Also you don't understand why the ideas of Martin Luther took such hold and why Protestants so to speak 'took over' in Northern Europe. The very name 'Reformation' implies they thought the Catholic Church had it all wrong before.

And, as you've found out, certain people today claim that is still the case! (Catholics. 'Got it all wrong', I mean.) Oh dear! So much to explain. I hardly know where to start.

Anyway, before we go any further, we have to get back to this business of how and why today's Catholics and Protestants (along with the population in general) differ in the way they use certain words. . .

Church for example. Could be the ancient building down the road, belonging to the Church of England, still with the Sovereign (at present the Queen) as its Head, according to the law of our land that dates all the way back to Henry VIII. Could be a building belonging to the Methodist Church, the Baptist Church, and so on. In fact 'church' can be a place of worship for any number of groups calling themselves Christians.

It can also refer to 'a group of believers in Christ' who have got together as 'a church' with a leader known as a pastor. Some of these groups belong to a larger group such as the Assemblies of God, while some are independent or 'free'. There are a simply enormous number of such 'churches' to be found all over the world in our day.

It could be also a building belonging to Catholics and referred to by us as 'the church' with a small 'c'. But when a Catholic says 'the Church' with a capital 'C', he or she means 'The Body of Christ' made up of the members of the 'One, Holy, Catholic, and Apostolic Church'.

In Britain we are referred to as 'the Catholic Church' or 'the Roman Catholic Church' or 'the Roman Church'. Although no longer officially persecuted, we can feel. . . well. . . let's just say 'not normal' in this country. Nevertheless, we are world-wide, and our Faith was handed down to us from the Apostles chosen by Christ himself.

So now you know! But please go on asking.

Your friend,
Auntie May

FOURTH LETTER

Dear William,

For two reasons I have decided to send you an extra letter.

I'd like first to go back to what you told me about your child-hood impressions of Christianity. I gather that what, in my day, used to be 'Scripture Lessons' were for you 'Religious Education', and had to cover all world faiths under the heading of 'comparative religion'.

The details about Christianity, you say, 'were factual rather than devotional', with St. Paul's missionary journeys coming across a bit like a lesson in ancient Geography. What a shame!

Your attention was drawn to Jesus' teaching but what you were told left you thinking of it as very hard to follow. I remember thinking that at school, too. It's true. It is actually impossible, relying on one's own strength, to live according to Jesus' Sermon on the Mount.[1]

Only the GRACE that God gives makes a person able to walk that road, and apparently you were not led to know that.

---

[1] Matthew 5:2 – 7:29

I find it very sad that no-one introduced you to the real Jesus who is ALIVE and is the only one able to supply that grace. Would you agree that's how it was? We can come back to the meaning of 'grace'.

The other reason for this letter is to do with Ascension Day. It is a special event in the Church's year, the day when the risen Jesus went back to his Father in heaven, leaving his chief followers, the Apostles, to await the coming of the Holy Spirit, the Paraclete[2] he had promised before he died.

We celebrate Ascension Day tomorrow. And to explain my letter heading: the 'Eve' of any such day, is the evening before, kept from 6 o'clock as part of the day itself. This is significant.

Following Ascension Day, we are encouraged to make a 'novena' (nine special days of prayer), because the Bible (which we Catholics, remember, tend to refer to as 'Scripture') tells us how the Apostles – together with *'Mary the Mother of Jesus'*[3] – were commanded to do just that same thing. During these days we, in our day, are awaiting a fresh outpouring of the Holy Spirit.

Why? Well, belonging to the Church is all about loving and serving God and those around us; and we need to be constantly

---

[2] John 15:26
[3] Acts 1:13-14

refreshed and empowered[4] for the task. And so at this time we think about, and pray for, the gifts of the Holy Spirit[5], preparing ourselves for a renewal of these gifts, first received by each member of the Church – as I hope to explain if you wish – in what we call the 'Sacraments' of Baptism and Confirmation.

Life is a journey, William. There is no standing still. We need to grow in holiness and in service of the Church and the world.

Meanwhile I have not forgotten that exams are coming up and you have revision to do. I shall now hold back until I hear from you that they are over.

Do please share what you are planning for the summer, won't you? Cuthbert and I are hoping for walks and picnics.

Now I must turn to reading the Scriptures that the Church gives us for Ascension and the blessed days leading up to the Holy Spirit's Feast of Pentecost. It is a favourite time of year for me. Perhaps I shall get as far as sharing with you what happened to make it that way. . .

Wishing you every success in the exams,

Your friend,
Auntie May

---

[4] John 16:13-15
[5] Isaiah 11:1-2

FIFTH LETTER

Dear William,

Of course I don't mind!! My novena is nearly completed now. So. . . the History exam is the last and is still a week away. You'd like me to say something about the Catholic priesthood, because it's always being stressed by your teachers that the Reformation taught 'the priesthood of all believers'.

Yes, that came from Martin Luther - also from Tyndale who translated the Bible into English. Both of them wanted to underline the importance of every baptised person. Notice I say 'underline' because what you have not been made aware of is that the Catholic Church has always claimed 'the priesthood of all believers'. You'll find the basis of that in the First Letter of Peter (2:5-9).

Here's a quote from something I wrote during my recent studies:

> '. . .every person baptised in the Catholic Church is cleansed from sin, becomes a child of God (an inheritor of eternal life) and is made prophet, priest and king by virtue of becoming a member of Christ's Body. . .The Sacrament of Baptism involves not only being baptised in water but also being anointed, first with the 'oil of

salvation' and afterwards with the 'oil of chrism', (the second of which is repeated only at Confirmation and when a person is seriously ill). Jesus, of course, is the eternal High Priest of the New Covenant (see the Letter to the Hebrews, esp.3:1).'

I should like to add so much more. . . but what you might need for the exam could be this:

Before his death Christ had made his Twelve Apostles priests, at what we know as the Last Supper: an occasion, by the way, that is in very truth, much more than a simple sharing of bread and wine.

In the final verses of St. Matthew's Gospel we find him commanding his Apostles to carry on his work of preaching the Gospel – the Good News – 'to the ends of the earth' and, as the Gospel of Luke says, 'to all nations'. This they did after Pentecost in the power and grace of the Holy Spirit.

Then, towards the end of their lives, they appointed BISHOPS from those who had been made priests by the Apostles through anointing and 'laying on of hands' (2 Tim1:6). The bishops ordained more priests ('presbyters') as their helpers.

Every Catholic bishop and priest can trace his priestly ordination back to the Apostles and so to Christ himself. It's true! It's called the APOSTOLIC SUCCESSION.'

What bishops and priests are ordained to do is a huge topic, which I am sure will crop up again, William, if you wish to know more. Let's see how it goes.

I'm praying you do well in all your exams, but naturally it's the History I'm thinking of most.

Your friend,
Auntie May

Sixth Letter

Dear William,

I wanted to reply when your postcard arrived from Venice, but you forgot to give me Martin and Richard's home address. I gather you spent several weeks with their family, including the holiday in Europe. What wonderful hospitality! They must be very good Christian people.

And you learned from them how to find your way around your Bible. Mostly the New Testament by the sound of it. Well, the New Testament is after all the Scripture of the New Covenant – of God with humanity – in Jesus Christ.

And it is where humanity met Jesus, 'the Word made flesh'. I drew your attention to that with my verses from John's Gospel and his First Letter, remember? And yet (the Church teaches) the Word and the Spirit were at work in a hidden way throughout the Old Testament, too.

Anyhow, you passed all your exams. I'm so glad!! 'What a mercy!' was what my grandmother used to say when her children wrote home with another exam behind them.

And you had the very question you thought might come up!

Your History teacher must have been impressed to have wanted to speak to you afterwards. Did you convince him? I'm sorry now that I didn't give you the source of the information about priesthood and the laying on of hands that we call 'ORDINATION'.

And perhaps I should have gone on to describe the task of the priesthood within the Church? Frankly, though, I reckoned it was more than you needed to know right then. We'll come to it, I hope.

I was once in Venice myself on my way to join a Mediterranean cruise, but that was before I was a Catholic and I never went into St. Mark's. If I had, I'm sure I would have been struck, like you, by the smell of incense, and the statues. Not surprisingly, the Christian family you were with only saw St. Mark's as a tourist attraction and thought its riches contrary to Jesus' teaching. And yet you tell me you found it peaceful and would have liked to linger. Perhaps I shall later be able to share with you what could well have been the reason. There is no doubt in my mind that GOD's LOVE must be there.

Anyway, you say you had a good time with your friends, and enjoyed going to their home church on the next two Sundays, after you all got back from the trip. You enjoyed the singing, but found the sermons long. Yes, they do tend to go on a bit. Main question is, were they helpful?

I gather you are now home again at your dad's place, keeping yourself well-occupied while he is away on business as he so often is. You say you are dividing your time between the garden and your much-loved carpentry workshop. I'm trying to picture both, and getting an imaginary scent of fresh roses from the one and that wonderful whiff of new-sawn wood from the other.

Do you cook for yourself as well?

And are you looking forward to your final year?

God bless!
Auntie May

SEVENTH LETTER

Field Cottage,

Oct. 13th. St. Edward the Confessor, King

Dear William,

Thank you so much for writing. I was thinking about you yesterday, hoping I would hear from you soon. Glad you are settled in and working hard.

Ah! So your History folks have moved you on to the 19th century! That's most likely in keeping with what you will find yourself teaching in a Primary School. Well I hardly dare to hope they will mention how – after centuries of persecution – Catholic worship was once more allowed in our country (in stages). It will be interesting to see if they do, and what they have to say about it.

Now. . . You'd like me to fill in the gaps in my earlier letters. I'll leave this letter open and see what I can do over the next couple of days.

OCTOBER 16TH
It's pouring with rain and Cuthbert's had to be content with what I call a mini-walk, so I've lit a fire to dry us both off and settled down to see to those gaps you mentioned.

1. WHY MY EMPHASIS ON JESUS AS WAY, TRUTH AND LIFE?
The short answer is, 'Because it says it all'.

Jesus is divine and human, God and Man, declared by the Church as having two natures in one Person. What does this mean?

As God, Jesus is, ever was, and ever shall be TRUTH and LIFE. As Man, he showed himself to be Truth and Life and also 'THE WAY'.

'The Way' was in fact the name given to the Faith before '*in Antioch the disciples were first called Christians*'.[1] We are Jesus' followers (disciples) and learn from him.

As I've said before, our life on earth is a journey; and obedient disciples – like the horses who ploughed the fields for our ancestors – 'walk on' as told. Seriously, obedience is at the heart of this following which we call 'discipleship'. We must LISTEN to Jesus, and do what he asks.

Our very being is a gift of God, as you will have learned by now from your earlier reading of the first two chapters of Genesis, as well as from your Bible as a whole, and from your Christian friends.

Then Jesus gives us 'New Life' in Baptism – the life of GRACE that comes to us through the Holy Spirit.

1 Acts 11:26

The subject of Baptism is one we have only touched on so far and is essential, but read John 3 to begin with. I am talking about the New Life that Jesus bought for us through his Death and Resurrection. That subject is at the heart of everything. I'm sure we shall come to look at it more closely.

2. ABOUT THE REFORMERS' TEACHING

I get the impression they preached that *now at last* people could learn from them the 'true Faith'? My reaction is *'Really*?!' This was 15 centuries after Christ!!!

And then – about some Christians of today having no time for Catholics. Yes, there is a link but that's not all. Much has happened since then. I'll do my best. . .

In fact, it seems the Reformers taught – and many still teach – that we should be guided by 'Scripture alone' and are saved by 'faith alone'. From all this comes the question you may be asked today: 'Have you been saved?'

The Church, on the other hand, teaches that 'faith and works' are necessary. No, I'm not saying we have to earn salvation. Jesus Christ has paid the price of our salvation by dying on the Cross, rising from the dead and ascending to his Father. But what we should do is 'show the fruits' of our faith, by our good works. Do please read the First Letter of St. Peter Chapter 1.

The Reformers were also keen to point out any lack of holiness in the Church of the time. And it is the same today. Protestants have a strong emphasis on living by one's faith, as I'm sure you are aware. The family who invited you on holiday will have shown you that.

Well, the Church, too, likewise drawing on Scripture, teaches love of God and of our neighbour and has strict moral standards. Yet with shame I have to admit we do have something to answer for, because some of those baptised into what is truly the One, Holy, Catholic, and Apostolic Church do not seem to have grasped its teaching, and some have even drifted away.

Maybe the reason is that we are taught as children, and my own view is that we should carry on learning as adults. That was one of the reasons for my recent studies, William. And they are helping me explain things to you.

However there have been great Saints (holy people) in the past and there are still many holy people in the Church today, some – like Mother Teresa of Calcutta – known to all the world; and thousands more known to God alone.

In our Britain today, anti-Catholic attitudes seem to me to be partly on the original Protestant grounds, and maybe even from the times when Catholics were not allowed in our country – although those times may be scarcely remembered, and English history books are quick to remind us that many Protestants were likewise put to death during the five-year reign of the Catholic daughter of Henry VIII, the so-called 'Bloody' Mary (1553–58). But still the Church of England came through as the established church in England, and so, it is often thought and spoken of by English people as 'The Church'.

One more thing. Of Catholics who were (only since the late 18th century) again allowed to practice the Faith here, I imagine not that many were descended from old English families. Instead the first public places of Catholic worship allowed were 'mission churches' with priests from Europe ('foreigners'!): and there were many Irish and Italians in the congregations.

After World War II came the first Polish Catholics and then some Catholics from the Caribbean islands, and now we have people from all over the world. All this makes the Church seem 'foreign'. And remember we are often called 'Roman' because the Pope is the Bishop of Rome, while the Queen of England is Head of the 'Church of England'!

William dear, I have to stop there. I need to get in more logs for the fire and make myself some lunch.

God bless you!
Auntie May

P.S. I've more than once heard it said that some 'churches' of today claim the True Faith was lost for centuries and came alive again at the Reformation. **What ?!**

Eighth Letter

Field Cottage,
Oct. 31st Hallowe'en

Dear William,

Well, here we are on the Eve of what used to be called 'All Hallows', now known as 'All Saints' (Nov.1st) And I feel I've got to say that this fuss about 'celebrating' Hallowe'en with its focus on things that are creepy, ugly and even downright evil, is all a nonsense. It came originally from *the fleeing away of wicked spirits* before the great Feast when the Church remembers all its holy people of the past, now Saints in heaven.

Now, just who do you reckon is behind the fact that 'All Saints'– which we Catholics keep as a 'Holy Day'– is now largely forgotten or ignored, and instead this false and foolish attention is given to the Eve (Hallowe'en)? Some might say it is commercial pressure. True, shops and businesses do benefit. But Christians should be aware that behind it is the Evil One, from whom the Lord himself taught us to pray to be delivered! Let us ask the Saints in heaven to join their prayers with the pilgrim Church on earth that GOODNESS may prevail.

It's true you will find All Saints Day in the calendar of the Church of England. Perhaps not kept by every parish but I believe they do have a service here in the village. I may hear the bell ringing in the morning as I set off in my car to get to Mass in town.

Sorry, William. It's late and I shall have to be up earlier than usual. Cuthbert has to have his walk before I set off. He doesn't keep Holy Days.

I've just realised you asked about the Sermon on the Mount. I'll make a note for next time.

May God bless and support you in all you do!
Your Auntie May

Ninth Letter

Dear William,

You asked about the Church's year, and why I head my letters with the names of Holy Days and Saints' Days. Well, that's not too hard to explain, though it will take a while.

I told you already that the Church has its own calendar. This marks the various seasons of the 'Liturgical Year', which begins with the four Sundays of Advent, leading up to Christmas. This year Advent is due to start next Sunday as 'Christ the King' marks the last Sunday of each Year.

The next Season is Christmas, which actually lasts longer than just the twelve days to the arrival of the Wise Men (the Feast of Epiphany, a word meaning 'revelation'). The Christmas Season actually ends with 'Candlemas', 'The Presentation of the Lord' in the Temple. I'll make a note to write to you on that splendid Feast.

Most people have heard of the Season of Lent – a disciplined time, they say, for giving up chocolate. It is actually the 40-day period leading up to Easter (an unfortunate name, by the way, taken from a pagan goddess!). Easter is when all Christians celebrate Christ's Death and Resurrection, and it varies year by year according to the moon, because these events are his 'Passover', and it all took place at the time of the Jewish Passover.

Now, to explain. . .I'll put this as simply as I can . . .

The book of Exodus tells how the Israelites were delivered from slavery in Egypt.[1] On that night they were to slaughter a lamb and eat it with bitter herbs and unleavened bread; they were to put its blood on the doorposts, and the angel of God, sent to slaughter all the firstborn of the Egyptians, would 'pass over' the People of God. This (the Church teaches) 'prefigured' the Passover of Christ, which delivers us from the slavery of sin.

You see, Jesus, by the shedding of his Precious Blood, has saved us from the slavery of sin. (Read I John 1: 5-7, William, and you will also find there 'light', 'life' and 'truth'. It all ties in.) And, as you well know, Jesus' Death was followed by his Resurrection, his Ascension to heaven, and the descent of the Holy Spirit at Pentecost – another Jewish feast, so named because it falls 50 days after Passover. Pentecost completes the Easter Season (Eastertide).

Your first letter to me arrived in Eastertide, I remember!

After Pentecost comes Trinity Sunday. The rest of the Year is covered by the 32 (sometimes 33) Sundays in Ordinary Time. It all follows from whenever Easter fell, you know. As I said, we

---

[1] Exodus 12:21ff.

end with 'Christ the King' after which we start again with Advent.

Meanwhile Saints' Days are marked according to the ordinary calendar. Each has its own date. This keeps all the many Christians of the One, Holy, Catholic and Apostolic Church, on the same track. That's what 'catholic' means, William, 'universal' (worldwide).

Oh dear! You wanted more on the Sermon on the Mount. Well, I already said it cannot be lived except by GRACE, and those who live by its Beatitudes[2] will also be persecuted, mark you! The same applies to all the teachings of the New Testament. They are only real and fully possible to those who are baptised into Christ, and living in the power of the Holy Spirit.

And now I'm going to 'put the cat among the pigeons' by adding, 'and guided by the Church' – a very important statement indeed, which needs to be taught properly so that it does not come across as if I were stating that 'Catholics have to do everything the Pope says', which is not at all what is meant.

The topic would take up a whole letter, I am sure. For now I'd rather point you to how the Lord told his disciples to pray in Matthew 6: 9-13 (also Luke 11:1-4). This is THE prayer for all who follow Christ. For that reason, it is essential to pray it with

---

[2] Matthew 5:1-12

God-given understanding. Sadly, it has been kind of 'deadened' for many of us by being said in a way that fails to bring out its depths. I'm sure I am not the only one to think that.

Listen, I can't wait to hear more of your doings. It's partly so that I know 'where you are at' and also because it is so lovely to have some fresh news to read on these dark winter nights. Even Cuthbert listens, when I read extracts. Believe that if you wish! It's not on the same level as what I'm saying about the Catholic Faith, though.

God bless you!
Auntie May

P.S. I notice you haven't mentioned Martin and Richard for a while or the Bible Study group.

TENTH LETTER

Dear William,

I think just ponder slowly and prayerfully those verses I gave you (the Lord's Prayer, which we Catholics usually refer to as the 'Our Father').

Note that in Luke's Gospel it was while Jesus was praying that the disciples asked him to teach them 'how to pray, as John the Baptist taught his disciples'.[1] Simply ask the Lord to teach you, too. And maybe ponder how he himself was 'put to the test' in the wilderness[2] after his Baptism by John in the Jordan. That is a typical subject for Lent, by the way, and a lot more profitable than just giving up chocolate!

I'm full of questions still, and hoping very much that you will feel like writing before the end of term, in spite of all you have on right now. I'm dying to know what you are making. Does it have to be a secret?

And how about your Christian contacts at college? That is where we started, isn't it? And, on the academic side, has anything been said about the return of Catholic worship to England?

---

[1] Luke 11:1
[2] Matthew 4:1-17; Mark 1:12-13; Luke 4:1-13.

I should so like to be able to imagine you at Christmas! I expect you will be with your dad. I hope there's heating in the workshop. The forecast says snow.

Looking forward to hearing more.
Your Auntie May

ELEVENTH LETTER

Field Cottage,
3rd Sunday of Advent

Dear William,

Your letter dated December 10th was delayed a little in the Christmas post but arrived this afternoon. I'm delighted. What a lot of news. And so kind of you to get back to me when you are preparing the stage for the pantomime and trying to finish your woodwork project.

Sorry, I had not realised that Martin left at the end of the last year. How nice that he's teaching near home, living with his family and going to his home church. Richard, you say, is still in his second year and you see him at Bible Study on Thursdays, when you can get there.

I got hold of a Good News Bible, by the way, and it certainly is easy to read. I'm saying that to encourage you to read it all you can. For my studies I had to use The New Jerusalem Bible, which is the one we hear read in church. I have the Pocket and Standard Editions, one for ordinary use and the other, rather heavy to handle, but with useful introductions to the books and large numbers of footnotes.

Your plan to revisit the Church of England at Christmas sounds a wonderful idea. I hope you recapture some of that sense of awe and wonder you felt as a child.

Have a happy time!

Love, Auntie May

Twelfth Letter

Field Cottage,
Jan 17th, St. Anthony, Abbot

Dear William,

I was so happy to hear about your lovely Christmas.

Alicia. What a pretty name! You didn't say much about her, only that you met her in the local supermarket and helped carry her shopping home. And then she offered to help you put up the crib the Vicar had asked you to fix for St. Mary's. I hope she dressed up warm. Those old buildings! Makes me shiver even to think about it. Did I tell you I belonged to the Church of England myself for a few years?

You went to the Christmas Eve service but did not see her there, and were disappointed. But did you, all the same, recapture the way you felt when you were a child?

I liked hearing how you and your father cooked lunch together. He seems in good health. I think of him as still young, you know. Well, compared with myself, he is.

The snow held off until after Christmas here, but came down heavily on New Year's Eve. So I didn't get to Mass for The

Solemnity of the Mother of God, which falls on the Octave of Christmas – to everyone else New Year's Day.

And we've been hugging the fire ever since. (That dog! He'd have it all to himself if he could.)

Is it Teaching Practice this term?

Happy New Year!

Love, Auntie May.

Thirteenth Letter

Field Cottage,
Feb. 2nd, The Presentation of the Lord

Dear William,

Ah! So her name is Alicia Mary and she had an Irish great-grandfather. If you'd told me her middle name before, I might have guessed where she worships. And the great-grandfather clinched it – although to be honest she didn't need to be of Irish descent. She could have been from anywhere in the world, as I told you before. You also found out she'll be eighteen in the summer just after she leaves school.

I'll share with you what came into my mind straight away. She's herself. One precious child of God, destined for heaven. I'm going to pray for her at Mass from now on. (For you, too, of course!)

Now, mind if I go back to filling in gaps? There's one from the very first letters each of us wrote. You said you wondered why the various fellowships and so on at your college did not 'join together' and I'd like to air that situation with you.

You see, I am surprised that nobody has tried to draw you in further and get you to join one or other of their churches. Perhaps people tend to hold back in college. Elsewhere, sooner or later, you'd get the usual question, 'Have you given your life to Christ?' You need to be clear about several things here.

You were baptised as a baby. That is what a Church of England 'Christening' is. Baptism is a 'one-off', William! It cannot be repeated. You already belong to the Father, the Son and the Holy Spirit. You have already been washed clean of 'original sin'[1] and claimed by the Holy Trinity, the one God.

Why am I telling you all this? Because some churches, – the Baptists for instance, who do not recognise infant Baptism – insist on 'total immersion' as an initiation into membership. I've even heard that some others dispense with Baptism altogether!

Yet Jesus commanded his Apostles to baptise, and in the Acts of the Apostles we read of whole households being baptised. The Church has always baptised both infants and adults, although the emphasis on one or the other has varied over the centuries.

Anyway, YOU are baptised already. No-one can change that. Now you have to search out a place to worship where you can grow in faith, hope and love, and learn what is God's plan for your life.

But meanwhile, I still want to add something about the pressure you might come under from the various churches you have come across so far.

[1] Genesis 3. The first sin, of Adam and Eve, left all of us much more likely to fall into temptation. Jesus sets us free.

I'm thinking in particular about the so-called 'altar call' that often follows the visit of an ardent preacher – a call to come forward and 'commit your life to Christ'.

Remember, the Bible is what all these Protestant churches claim to go by. Yes, of course it is true that God speaks there. Contrary to some Protestant opinion, Catholics also know with certainty that in and through the Scriptures we hear the Word of God. (As the Church teaches) the Author of all Holy Scripture, both Old and New Testaments, is the HOLY SPIRIT. And, believe it or not, Catholic Bibles include more books than Protestant Bibles – seven more, to be exact.

'Then what's the problem?' you may ask. Well, you would be wise to be aware of something else you might have to face from these enthusiastic Christians (many of them anti-Catholic as well):

Let's imagine that, in an attempt to convert you, they quote you John 3:16. (I've pointed you to John 3 already. Look again at verse 16).

And then they will almost certainly say that you need to be 'BORN AGAIN'. And when you respond to that – as the crowds responded to Peter on Pentecost Day being 'cut to the heart'[2]

---

[2] Acts 2: 37

- they will likely say, 'You must acknowledge Jesus as your Lord and Saviour and welcome him into your heart.' Those words do not appear like that in the Bible, William, and it could be said that this is a 'formula' (based maybe on Rom 10: 8-10 & Jn 17:3). What Peter in fact replied was, *'you must repent of your sins and be baptised.'*[3]

Now please, dear William, straight away pick up on John 3 again, but earlier, at v.3, and find Jesus' answer to Nicodemus. The Bible says being *'born again'* involves *'water and the Spirit'*. Water and the Spirit were there at creation and continue to appear together throughout Scripture, as at Jesus' own Baptism. I ought to explain why I've said all this today.

Yes, it was certainly to emphasise that you are baptised already. But it was also to remind you that your Christian friends at college, *don't agree with each other*. You said from the start that you were confused by this. And their various places of worship don't agree either, you see, even though all say that they go by the Bible.

Would you wish to join any of those churches, do you think? If not, then certainly you could defend yourself by saying you are already baptised into the Church of England.

I can tell you from experience it has a wide range of belief within

---

[3] Acts 2:38

it, but I shan't go more into that now as this letter is far too long.
And you are so busy with your teaching. I know what it can be
like. I have been a teacher (as I daresay you can tell!).

I must get ready now as it's a friend's birthday and we are going
out for tea at a café in town. Cuthbert will be delighted. He can
hog the fire.

God bless you, dear William!

Love from,
Auntie May

Fourteenth letter

Dear William,

I'm sorry if you had expected to hear from me sooner. It's felt like a long time for me, too, but I decided not to write when you had so much to do. And then came your letter about your holiday plans. Exciting!

Meanwhile Lent is practically over and Easter nearly upon us. This is such a special time. During the three days known as the Easter Triduum – the Thursday of the Last Supper, Good Friday, and then the Easter Vigil on Saturday night – we follow our Redeemer on the journey he made to save us.

Before that, on the first three days of Holy Week we think of him dividing his time chiefly between Jerusalem – where the first three Gospels tell that he cleansed the Temple[1] – and Bethany, where he could be with his friends, Martha, Mary and Lazarus. His disciples do not seem to realise what is to happen so soon. John's Gospel, the last to be written, makes it clear that Jesus knows his 'Hour'[2] is near.

---

[1] Matthew 21:12-13; Mark 11:15-17; Luke 19:45-46.
[2] Only John's Gospel uses this word, (John 13:1) for Christ's Passion and Death.

There is much to speak of regarding Holy Week, but instead I'm going to share with you an earlier passage of Scripture where the Old and New Testaments come together, and where – so Luke tells us – Jesus' forthcoming Passion is spoken of.[3] Even then, the three Apostles, Peter, James and John – present with Jesus on the mountain at his 'Transfiguration' – fail to understand.

Yet here the presence of the Holy Trinity is revealed. Jesus is seen glorified in his humanity; the Father's Voice is heard claiming him as his Beloved Son and saying *'Listen to him'*; and the Holy Spirit descends as a *'cloud'* (*the shekinah*, which, as we read in the Old Testament, had led the Israelites in the desert, had come down on Moses' Tent of Meeting and had later filled the Temple of Solomon).

I'm trusting, you see, that this will show you how everything Jesus went through was within God's plan.

As we read in John's Gospel, the last to be written, Jesus had earlier declared,

'No-one takes (my life) from me; I lay it down of my own free will, and as I have power to lay it down, so I have power to take it up again; and this is the command I have received from my Father.'(Jn 10:18)

Now. You are going to go to the Church of England this Easter –

---

[3] Luke 9:28-36

to St. Mary's. You say your father won't be with you, but at least he can't object now you're an adult.

My hope is that you can make a good journey through these precious days of recalling the Passion, Death and Resurrection and that Jesus himself will speak to you about how and why he suffered for you.

(Forgive me for saying if you already know this, but, as you were never 'confirmed' in the Church of England, I suppose you will not be able to 'take Communion', as they say? That was certainly the rule in my time.)

Perhaps I should share with you now, that out of any who decide to join us in the Catholic Church at the Easter Vigil, only the unbaptised – known from the very beginnings of the Church as 'catechumens' – receive the initial Sacrament, Baptism; while those already baptised are welcomed, 'received' and 'admitted to the Sacraments'. There is a lengthy period of preparation for all before this happens – and the usual time for 'coming into the Church' is at the Easter Vigil. Such a beautiful occasion! I wish I could claim that many will be joining us this year but at least there are some. It adds so much to this splendid ceremony – the first Mass of Easter – when the new Paschal candle is lit and we sing the first 'alleluias' since Ash Wednesday, the beginning of Lent.

I've just time catch today's post. I'm also planning an extra letter to you this week. I'd better get that in the post tomorrow,

I suppose, or it will not reach you before the Good Friday Bank
Holiday.

May God bless your Eastertide!

Love, Auntie May

FIFTEENTH LETTER

Field Cottage,
Tuesday of Holy Week

Dear William,

I've chosen a strange topic for today. At first sight you may think it's not about Holy Week at all. Maybe I was inspired by the name of your church, St. Mary's. Or maybe I was thinking of your hope of seeing Alicia Mary again during the holiday, when she comes to visit her grandmother.

Only twice have I mentioned our 'Mother Mary' in what is nearly a year since we started writing. I could have chosen to talk about her at Christmas at the birth of her Baby Jesus. Pretty much everyone knows her role in Bethlehem, I should think. But it all began in Nazareth when the Angel Gabriel announced that she, a virgin, was to conceive our Saviour by the overshadowing of the Holy Spirit. It is Luke who gives us this account. His is the longest of the so-called 'infancy narratives' about the Birth of John the Baptist and the Birth of Christ - while Matthew gives us the Epiphany.

Yes, it's a big leap from Bethlehem to the events of Holy Week: the Passion, Death and Resurrection of that same Jesus, Mary's divine Son.

So why choose to talk about Mary at this time?

Well, when Luke was writing of her as Mother of the Christ, he told of the Child's Presentation in the Temple after 40 days. There she and Joseph were met by Simeon and Anna – two faithful Jewish people whom the Holy Spirit allowed to recognise their promised Saviour (their Messiah). Simeon also prophesied,

> *'This child is set for the rise and fall of many in Israel'* and to Mary he said, *'. . .and a sword shall pierce your own soul also, that the thoughts of many shall be laid bare.'*[1]

How has Mary come into my letters? Well, once was about her presence during the first 'novena' of prayer from the Ascension to Pentecost, remember? Acts tells us that *'Mary the Mother of Jesus'* was there. And on Pentecost day (the Church teaches) she became 'Mother of the Church', which is the Body of her Son. We are thus her children.

On New Year's Day we Catholics are all at Mass (weather permitting) celebrating the Solemnity of the Mother of God. That title was proclaimed for her at the Council of Ephesus in 431 AD, when the Bishops of the Church met to deal with certain heresies.[2] The Church said Christ was (and is) both God and Man. And Mary is 'Mother of God'.

---

[1] Luke 2:34-35
[2] False teachings

The Gospels, too, portray Mary as worthy of yet another name. Luke tells how her cousin Elizabeth, mother of John the Baptist, said – while Jesus, like her own child, was still unborn – *'Who am I that the mother of my Lord should come to me?'* Then, *'Blessed is she who believed that the promises made to her would be fulfilled.'*

We, as disciples, must believe in the promises of God. Mary is therefore given us as the First Disciple. And read for yourself her words to the servants at the Wedding in Cana (John 2:5). She speaks those words to all disciples of her Son throughout the ages.

I know. I haven't answered the question, 'Why write of her at this time?' Why at this stage of the Liturgical Year, when everyone is focused on our Lord and Saviour, Jesus Christ, and his great Act of Redemption? Well, at the Crucifixion, Simeon's prophecy was fulfilled, and *'a sword . . .pierce(d) her own soul also'*. Mary at the foot of the Cross earned another of her titles, Mother of Sorrows.

It may be hard for you as a young man – even with your own past share of sorrow – to feel a mother's heartache. Then think instead of how Jesus felt her pain, and yours. He suffered for you on the Cross.

And then, what JOY! THE LORD IS RISEN!

Happy Easter, William!

Love from your Auntie May.

Sixteenth Letter

Dear William,

You've had a long wait for this. I've never even thanked you for your news of what happened at Easter. So sorry!

Actually, I've been looking after Cuthbert. On one of our walks he fell over the edge of a disused quarry. He was lucky to have got away with a broken leg and possible concussion. It was still cold at the beginning of May and I had to keep our fire going while the poor animal was still getting over it. (Well, that was my excuse!)

Now. . . your letter. It was so interesting to hear about the Good Friday procession through the town, with all churches involved. And how nice that Alicia suddenly joined you for the hymns in the market-place, this year led by the Methodist minister.

I gather you and she saw quite a bit of each other during the holiday. You even went to her Gran's place.

Ah yes! The statues in her house. Did you recognise Mary? Was she in white with a blue sash? If so she was 'Our Lady of Lourdes'. And the other figure you described would be the Sacred Heart of Jesus.

They each represent a particular VISION, William.

I'm going to be extremely brief here . . .

Jesus first. He appeared in that way to St. Margaret Mary in 1673
– as you said, 'standing with one hand indicating that his heart
is on fire.' The Saint was given a very hard time indeed when
she tried to carry out his wishes! But devotion to the Sacred
Heart has since spread worldwide and has its own Holy Day:
the Solemnity of the Most Sacred Heart of Jesus.

The Virgin Mary first appeared to St. Bernadette in Lourdes in
1858. Again no-one believed Bernadette at first and she had a
tough time of it, but Mary said some words about herself that
made the Church finally accept the apparition. (More on that in
a moment.)

It is easy, really. The statues simply represent the aspects of our
devotion to Our Lord and to his Mother (Our Lady) that God
especially wished his people to understand from that time on.
In the first case, God wanted to remind the world of just how
much Jesus loves us and that we should believe in and honour
this love much more. The statue of the Sacred Heart remains so
that we don't forget.

In the second case, he wanted the world to know for certain –
something that had been held since much earlier times – that
Mary was indeed created 'free from original sin' in order to
become the Virgin-Mother of his Son, Jesus Christ. The Pope,

Pius IX, had not long before declared this truth as 'dogma', that is 'essential to the Faith'.

You have led me into deep waters here, William. These are the things that, as a Protestant, I was likely to be told were 'inventions' of that 'terrible institution' called the Roman Catholic Church!! Can you believe that even quite recently I have heard the Pope still spoken of as the Anti-Christ? *Really?!*

I gather that you kept your questions (about the statues) to yourself. Later you told Alicia about our exchange of letters, but all she said was, 'Why did she call her dog Cuthbert?'!

So I think I'll end this letter by fielding that one, for her sake.

St. Cuthbert (634-687A.D.) was a saintly Anglo-Saxon monk and priest of the Northumbrian monasteries of Melrose and Lindisfarne. He wished to remain a hermit of the Farne Islands but later on reluctantly allowed himself to be consecrated as Bishop, then travelled far and wide among the poorer people of his time, performing many miracles. But in the end he went back to continue as a hermit until his death. His splendid Life was written by the Venerable Bede, himself famous for his Ecclesiastical History of the English People (c.731). Cuthbert's body was moved more than once on account of the invading Danes but was eventually brought to Durham Cathedral where it has its own peaceful shrine. I loved to pray there when I lived near enough to travel there and back in a day.

Saint Cuthbert, like St. Francis of Assisi in later times, lived close to birds and animals and they obeyed him. So I hoped he wouldn't mind lending his name to my dog.

With so much else to say, you hardly found space to tell me that you enjoyed the Easter services at St. Mary's, especially the hymns. That's good.

Well, with the dog now on the mend, I should be able to get back to answering you more promptly.

Oh, wait a bit. Another thing to tell you. I'm going start computer lessons! If I make progress, I'll tell myself I can afford a PC and my typewriter can join me in retirement.

God bless you, dear William!

Love, Auntie May

Seventeenth Letter

Dear William,

Well, here we are again at that wonderful time when the Holy Spirit descended on the Apostles – the Birthday of the Church. I'm going to write about the Holy Spirit but from another angle, because I promised to share with you why this day is so special for me personally.

I told you I spent some years in the Church of England. As I would have said then – it was while I was a student, like you – I 'became an Anglican'. I was baptised at the age of twenty-one.

I said 'an Anglican' because I was brought in by our University Chaplain who was what people often call 'High Church'. As I said before, the Church of England embraces a wide spread of belief and practice. (One of the 'side-effects' of the differences is that no-one can tell you what sort of service you will have if you attend a C of E church while on holiday.) The 'Low Church' parishes have services that are more like those of the Methodists. That leaves anything between High and Low as a sort of 'middle of the road'?? Where does St. Mary's fit, I wonder?

What was I before I was an Anglican? Well many of my ancestors had belonged to what was for a long time called The

Society of Friends - more widely known as Quakers - and my mother, who had been brought up C of E (Low Church) by her branch of the family, chose the Quakers instead.

I therefore began with Sunday School at the Meeting House when I was six, and the Quaker way of worship was all I knew until I went away to college. It gave me the advantage of reading the Bible, and even learning many passages of the Scriptures by heart. In the Sunday Meeting for Worship, the members simply spend an hour waiting on God in silence, unless the Holy Spirit moves an individual to stand up and 'minister' by sharing a thought or experience, or reading from the Bible.

So the reason I've mentioned my upbringing was to explain my love of the Holy Spirit, also my love of Scripture, and my love of silence (which very many Catholics share).

The Friends' Meeting for Worship taught me silence, but we also had hymns at my school. Some of them I still have a chance to sing today. Not many people realise, I think, that the words of the well-known hymn, *Dear Lord and Saviour of Mankind* are a poem written by John Greenleaf Whittier, an American Quaker. Yes, our life on earth is a journey, but when we move on we take with us our personal experience of God, who is with us even from conception, as Psalm 139 makes clear.

ABOUT PENTECOST DAY

As on very many days, but especially on the great Feasts, the

Church shares the same Liturgy worldwide. This expresses our UNITY.

The Scripture Readings on any day belong to that part of the Mass known as the Liturgy of the Word. Readers from the congregation will have been chosen to read. At most Masses, one of these comes up and reads the First Reading, which is from the Old Testament. Then follows the Responsorial Psalm, which may be said or sung, the congregation joining in the Response. On Sundays and Holy Days there is a Second Reading (mostly read by a different reader). This is from anywhere in the New Testament other than the Gospels, and is followed by the singing of the Alleluia. Then the priest reads the Gospel and gives a Homily (a short sermon) on this, bringing in all the readings for the day. Let me say right now: this pattern goes back to the first century, the earliest days of the Church.

Why am I telling you all this? Well, for one thing, I'm pointing to how different this pattern of worship is from what you may experience in some other churches, say those where the pulpit and pastor take central place, and the worship for the day is the pastor's choice, likewise the homily or sermon. Have you noticed the lack of an altar, by the way? That's a topic for another time, though.

Today I've only told you about the first part of the Mass, the Liturgy of the Word. Why? Because I'd like to list the Scriptures chosen for Pentecost. These will give you an insight into how much of the Bible the Church lays before her children, especially when I tell you that Sunday Masses run on a three-year cycle (A, B, and C) and Weekday Masses on a two-year cycle (I and II)! I can find them all in my book (called a Missal) and read them for myself as well as hearing them at Mass.

I find in my Missal that there is, for the Eve of Pentecost, an EXTENDED FORM Vigil Mass, which is a very grand affair with lots of instructions as to how it is to be celebrated. (Again, this is to preserve unity).

It has more Readings than usual. Here they are:
> Genesis 11:1-9;
> Exodus 19:3-8, 16-20;
> Ezekiel 37:1-14;
> Joel 3:1-5.

The SIMPLE FORM of the Vigil Mass, says to choose just one of these as the usual First Reading. The Second Reading is Romans 8:22-27, followed by the Gospel, John 7:37-39.

At the 'Mass during the Day' (Year A) the First Reading is, of course, Acts 2 :1-11; while the Second is from Corinthians 12 (vv.3-7,12-13), where St. Paul points out,

'In the one Spirit we were all baptised.'

So here we are, back on the subject of Baptism. How important it is!

Note that St. Paul says (in verse 3),

> *'No-one can say 'Jesus is Lord' unless he is under the influence*
> *of the Holy Spirit.'*

(The Church teaches) that everyone who is baptised in the Name of the Father, Son and Holy Spirit – not just in the Name of Jesus, notice – is a 'Christian'. No, I did not say all belong to the One, Holy, Catholic and Apostolic Church.

Why do some such Christians condemn us?

You will begin to understand, I feel, once I begin to explain about the true heart of the Mass, – the 'source and summit' – as this will bring us back to that 'huge topic' we left behind a whole year ago: the PRIESTHOOD.

I'm talking here about what Catholic bishops and priests are ordained to do, which was more than you needed to know for your exam. I can tell you right away that it all follows from that APOSTOLIC SUCCESSION I told you about at the time.

You asked after Cuthbert. Yes, he's back to his usual self, thank you. Not as obedient to me as he might have been to the dear Saint he's named after, but then. . . I'm no Saint!

Work hard, William, and I'm sure you'll do well. Is the project done?

Love, Auntie May

Eighteenth Letter

Dear William,

I'm guessing the only reason I've not heard from you is that you are busy revising. Besides, my last letter was long and gave you lots of suggestions for your Bible reading.

Let me say right away that I'm making good progress with the Computer Class. It runs twice a week at the Community Centre in town and I've time for a little shopping between daily Mass and the class – which reminds me to answer a question from one of your earlier letters. Yes, we do have Mass daily. Any day that falls in Ordinary Time and is neither part of a Season, nor a Feast Day, nor a Saint's Day is a 'Feria' and has Readings belonging to Years I or II. These follow through from one day to the next.

But today is Trinity Sunday. It is a time for dwelling on the 'mystery' of the ONE God, in THREE PERSONS – Father, Son and Holy Spirit.

I've read that Muslims sometimes accuse Christians of believing in Three Gods. That is not so. God is still the One God who revealed himself to the People of Israel. The word 'person' in English is misleading because it seems to mean 'an individual' but 'Person' here has more the meaning of the Greek, I am told.

I'm no Greek scholar, though.

What really matters is that the 'Three' share ONE LOVE. This makes such sense. Love implies 'someone to love'. Yes, God loves us – but that is his choice. To be the SOURCE of all love he must have LOVE within Himself.

Jesus has told us, 'The Father loves the Son'. Yes, you will have read it in John Chapter 3 (v.35). And, in an attempt to try and 'pin down' what one might call 'un-pin-down-able' (if such a word existed) – i.e. the mystery of God – the Church tells us the Holy Spirit is 'the Love between the Father and the Son' but is still a 'Person' (in the Greek sense), and all Three within the Godhead are equally 'God.'

God cannot be contained in language!!! Let the scholars handle the theology, while people like your Auntie May accept and worship.

Do you know any hymns of John Henry Newman, William? He wrote the one that begins, 'Lead, kindly Light . . .'and also the one that has as its first verse :

> 'Firmly I believe and truly,
> God is Three and God is One,
> And I next acknowledge duly
> Manhood taken by the Son.'

That hymn will have been sung in many churches this morning.

Well, those which have a 'calendar', that is. I may be wrong but I think other churches tend to be governed by their pastor's choice.

Yes, (the Church teaches) the Trinity is to be believed in by all Christians. That actual word does not appear in Scripture, but Father, Son and Holy Spirit are all three spoken of by Jesus and are there together in the final verses of Matthew's Gospel. Eventually the Church came to understand more fully hence the word 'Trinity'.

I do find it a help, you know, to ponder on Genesis 1:26, and also on Abraham's encounter with the 'three' who visited him by the oak of Mamre in Genesis 18, and before whom he 'bowed to the ground'. Looking at those verses in the Good News Bible, however, I notice a certain subtlety is lost in the easy narrative style.

There is a Russian ikon that captures the Abraham scene in depth. Many people have a copy in their homes, as I do here. God speaks to the heart through ikons and this one is special. Let me point out right now that we all have to make the journey from mind to heart – some call it 'the longest journey'. Children manage it most easily. Don't the Scriptures tell us so? Take, for instance, Psalm 131. And how about the words of Jesus himself: *'In truth I tell you, unless you change and become like little children you will never enter the kingdom of Heaven.'?* We all need the awe and wonder you felt at Christmas as a child.

I intended this to be a short letter because you are once again revising for exams. But today's Feast demanded attention.

Wishing you every blessing!

Your Auntie May

P.S. If you are in touch with Alicia, please tell her I pray for her every day. I'm also wondering if I will ever meet either of you. Maybe sometime.

NINETEENTH LETTER

Dear William,

In line with this great and beautiful Feast, I am setting out to tell you some 'serious stuff' here. May the Lord himself give you the necessary understanding!

Yes, today's Feast always overwhelms me. It constitutes a Holy Day when Catholics are 'obliged' to attend Mass, even though it takes place on a Thursday. In countries where the majority of Christians are Catholic it is a 'day off'. (Well it used to be. Whether it still is in these highly secular times – when work, which should sit alongside worship, is inclined to come before it – I'm not so sure.)

The Feast is actually a 'Solemnity of the Lord' and its English title is, 'The Most Holy Body and Blood of the Lord.' It was instituted, I believe, in the 13th Century as an additional focus on Christ's supreme GIFT OF HIMSELF on Holy Thursday, the night of the Last Supper.

What Jesus gave the apostles then . . .and gives us now. . .was his own Body and Blood to eat and drink!

Dear William, you simply must read John 6 and find out for

yourself about his teaching, his command, his promise. And how many could not take it! Many couldn't then, and many can't today.

There are three Gospel passages that give us an account of what we call 'the institution of the Eucharist'. But Paul's Letters were around before the Gospels. So today I am going to talk about Jesus' words in Paul's First Letter to the Corinthians (11:23 ff.)

Now, (the Church teaches) that when Jesus said, '**This is my Body**' and, '**This is my Blood**' he meant what he said! That is why, in the verses of I Corinthians 11 leading up to v. 23, St. Paul is 'telling the Corinthians off' for not taking seriously this greatest gift of our Lord and Saviour. This is indeed a most serious thing. (The Church teaches) that the Mass is 'the source and summit of our Faith'.

The Mass is at the centre of what bishops and priests are ordained to do. Only a bishop or priest may 'celebrate' the Mass, – saying the Eucharistic Prayer in which the solemn words of Christ are repeated and his Sacrifice on the Cross is 'shown forth'. As the 'celebrant' thus repeats Christ's words, the elements of bread and wine become his Body and Blood. In them is the 'life' he is speaking of in John 6.

This is indeed the heart of the Mass; and is why the Mass as a whole, is not 'a service'. It is not *what we do for God*, but *what God does for us* through the priest, acting '*in persona Christi*' (standing in for Christ himself).

I told you before, didn't I? Each bishop or priest has had his role handed down to him in a direct line from the Apostles, and thus from Jesus himself. Yes! The APOSTOLIC SUCCESSION. Why the capital letters? Because it is the reason for the Authority of the Church.

The Bishops, the Shepherds of the Church, with the Pope – the Successor of Simon Peter – as their Chief Shepherd, make up what is called the Magisterium. The teaching of the Church depends upon that structure, as Scripture shows us Jesus Christ said it should (John 20:19-22).

'As the Father sent me, so I am sending you,' (v.21). 'I have prayed for you, Simon, that your strength may not fail. And once you have recovered, you in turn must strengthen your brothers.' (Luke 21:31-32)

And so we come to Mass on this beautiful Feast to praise God as we always do; to hear the Scriptures; to offer our gifts and ourselves in thanksgiving; to see and hear the priest carry out Jesus' command in the Eucharistic Prayer; to receive Christ's Body and Blood, and then go forth to do his Will in our lives.

My love to you, William!

Auntie May

TWENTIETH LETTER

Field Cottage.
The Most Sacred Heart of Jesus

Dear William,

This lovely Solemnity falls on a Friday. But before I talk about that – and you already know something about it because of Gran's statue – I need to pay attention to your news.

So you've applied to teach at a Prep School not too far from home. I hope there really is a chance you may be able to run some woodwork classes with the older pupils as well as the usual range of subjects with your own Form of 8-year-olds. Won't they want you in the evenings and at weekends to supervise boarders? I mean, will you really have much time to help your dad with the garden and spend time in your own workshop?

But first there's the summer holiday. What an exciting plan! As usual, I have lots of questions. . . Sorry, William, I'm being nosy again. Writing to you has been like having a great-nephew, you know. (But will you want to carry on corresponding after your final exams, I wonder? You are going to be very busy.)

Devotion to the Sacred Heart is a way for many to say that they love and trust JESUS above all things. We say, 'Sacred Heart of Jesus, I place all my trust in You!'

Some Religious Orders (monks and nuns, that is,) are consecrated to the Sacred Heart; there are 'Sacred Heart parishes'; and
married couples can dedicate themselves and their families, and
have a picture inscribed with their names to hang in their house.

You have had so much from me lately that I am going to stop
short at this point. I just want to add that I am ordering my own
computer soon! Wait and see. . . Meanwhile, it's time for more
walks and picnics while the days are longer. Must remember to
order more logs, though. They are much cheaper in the summer.
Best wishes for the exams,

and much love from your friend,

Auntie May

PART II

TO A MAN SEEKING
TRUE LIFE IN CHRIST

LETTER ONE

Dear William,

I was so pleased to hear from you again, and have your school's address.

The first thing to say is thank you for the wonderful surprise! Fancy giving me your 'project piece'! I've always wanted an oak bookcase and, believe me, my books are loving it.

Glad to hear that your teaching is going well. It is not surprising that you enjoy the woodwork classes best, especially after your adventure in Canada and all that you learned from your Uncle Jack. Such valuable experience. I get the feeling you'd like to have stayed longer. Will you be going again?

I have to admit that I thought our exchange about matters of Christian belief had probably come to an end, but now it seems you want *more than ever* to ask me questions about the Catholic Church.

First there's your friendship with Alicia and her Gran, and then there are the many questions that arose after you discovered Uncle Jack's wife (Elisabeth, isn't it?) is a Catholic and hails from Montreal. Then the visit to their son who now lives there, and Mass in French!

Now . . . let's have a plan. I've got going on my PC and should be able to produce some notes that will prove helpful. I can even email you from time to time and send extra materials as an attachment. But I'd rather hear from you first about your questions, so today I'm typing on the PC but printing out and so this letter is going in the post as usual.

When we were writing to each other before, while you were still a student, you asked about SAINTS. Your friends were insisting that 'we are *all* saints'. Yes, the Bible speaks that way of 'the baptised' living here on earth. However, there are also those who have reached heaven and are known to have been very holy while on earth. In Hebrews (12:1) these are spoken of as '*so many witnesses in a great cloud all around us*' and these are watching us '*run the race*' (2 Timothy 4:7). They belong to the Church Triumphant. We belong to the Pilgrim Church, because we are still on our journey through this earthly life.

I think I told you about how I had just completed some studies when we started writing to each other? Well, I believe some excerpts from what I wrote then might be a help to you. I'll know better what to choose when I hear what you want to ask me.

But meanwhile, here is something (photocopied) about a favourite Saint of mine, St. Joseph. Yes! I'm speaking of THE St. Joseph, chosen by God to be husband of Mary and Christ's father-figure here on earth. Joseph the carpenter!

All the very best to you, William, and God's blessing on your work!

Your friend, Auntie May.

P.S. May I have your email address, please? Mine is rmayfield96@_____

'ATTACHMENT' 1B: (Taken from one of my essays)
INTRODUCTION TO THE SAINTS IN HEAVEN, WITH
SPECIAL MENTION OF ST. JOSEPH
We Catholics are fortunate in our certainty that, while on our journey through this life (see Hebrews 13:14), we are surrounded by a *'great cloud of witnesses'* (Heb 12:1)— the Saints who have *'run the race'* (2 Tim 4:7) and who, the Church assures us, have through Christ conquered death and are now before the throne of God in heaven. . .

THAT SPECIAL SAINT
Gradually - or sometimes even quite suddenly - one particular saint comes to feel like a friend. God knows exactly which saint(s) he wishes to stand by you — at a certain time or even throughout your life, to encourage you. . .and pray for you before his throne.

ST JOSEPH - A PERSONAL TESTIMONY

First acquaintance

I 'got to know' St. Joseph at an extremely difficult time in my life. Both my parents had died by the time I married. Some months later, I decided, through the example of my husband and his family, to 'come into the Church'. This I did, but only six weeks later my husband lost his life in a tragic accident. So I was now a young widow, heart-broken, and seeking God's Will for my life.

Some while later I found myself lodging with a very devout, retired lady. We lived right next to the Catholic Church . . .and we used to be out of bed soon after 7.00 am to be at Mass!

One day, this lady gave me a 'prayer card'. It explained a special and rather different kind of Novena to St. Joseph. It came from a certain Rev. Louis Lallement SJ who had lived some 400 years before. Instead of the usual long prayer addressing the Saint, - with somewhere in the middle '(Here make your petition)'- this one demanded four meditations each day on the life of St. Joseph:

> *His faithfulness to Grace*
> *His faithfulness to the Interior Life*
> *His love of the Blessed Virgin Mary*
> *His love of the Christ Child*

Each time one should 'Think, thank God, and ask'. And below, printed in red, were these words: 'You want to be quite sure that you want what you are praying for as you are certain to receive it.'

This Novena was just right for me as a former Quaker, not taught to 'say prayers' but only to read the Bible and to worship in silence, waiting on the Holy Spirit. (I had retained these preferences when baptised as an Anglican at University.) So right away, card in hand, I started praying for 'a deepening of my spiritual life' and gained much PEACE. I was clearly being enriched by God, through St. Joseph's example, his prayers and his loving care. The grace is always from the Lord.

I was soon able to purchase a statue of St. Joseph carrying the Christ Child. It kept me close to this wonderful saint, and it was his protection I now began to be aware of, while contemplating his virtues of obedience, humility and purity. I 'felt safe' with him and began to look to him to pray for me as I sought God's guidance.

I have to admit that, at the start, I scarcely knew who St. Joseph was. I knew he was there in the stable at Christmas and in paintings of 'The Flight into Egypt'. He was there in his carpenter's workshop in Nazareth when Jesus – Son of God but spoken of as 'son of Joseph'– was growing up.

No words of Saint Joseph being recorded in the Gospels, it is his presence and his actions that speak for him. The first two Novena meditations pointed me to St. Joseph's silence and drew me into that silence. The second two were a lesson in obedience and love – and cause for thanksgiving.

Learning more about St. Joseph helped me to praise God. I

found out about the saint's descent from Abraham and King David; and how — being that 'just man' (Mt 1:19) chosen by God to be the chaste Spouse and Guardian of the Mother of Jesus — he thus linked the Christ Child to the Old Testament promise of a Messiah; and as legal Guardian he was called upon to name the Child 'Jesus', acting towards the Son of God as 'earthly father', protector, provider and teacher.

From being 'Guardian of the Holy Family', he became known as 'Protector of Families'; as also 'of Virgins'. He is also known as 'Patron of the Dying' by virtue of having died before Christ's Passion, Death and Resurrection, traditionally 'in the arms of Jesus and Mary'; and in more recent times he has been declared 'Patron of the Universal Church' .

Meanwhile, I thanked God for St. Joseph's protection of me, and the example of his virtues, and continued to ask his intercession.

MY MIRACLE THROUGH ST. JOSEPH
The next Christmas I made a new friend, a widower. I spent the holiday with his family as housekeeper! We started to correspond. Then I got work in Ireland from January to July, after which I went back to teaching.

The school was 'St. Joseph's' as was the Parish Church.

I found myself wondering if my new friendship would lead to marriage. So I decided to make my special Novena to ask: 'Please show me if I am to marry this man or if this is not

God's Will.' Being still a relatively new Catholic, it didn't dawn on me that the Novena would end on March 19th, St. Joseph's Day!!

I made the last meditation in the church that evening, went home *and received a proposal of marriage over the phone!* We married that summer and had over 30 years together. Now I often find myself thinking that if I have to die alone, I shall be all right because 'Daddy Joseph' will be with me!

May God be praised in his Saints! Amen.

LETTER TWO

4th Nov. St. Charles Borromeo

Dear William,

I am so sorry the senior master is causing you stress. I can well understand this is taking you back to very sad times, and the eczema is also making the woodworking classes difficult. I do hope you can get the right ointment soon.

Regarding St. Joseph. Well, there was devotion to him in the Church from the earliest days. I have a prayer that claims it was discovered 'in the fiftieth year of Our Lord. . .'

March 19th was kept as his Feast in some areas from the 10th Century, and was made universal in the 16th Century. Yes, devotion to him increased from the time of the Reformation, when the great St. Teresa of Avila wrote of his unfailing answers to her prayers.

Since he was declared Patron of the Universal Church (1870), more people than ever ask for his guardianship of their lives, their families, and their work. In 1955, Pope Pius XII gave the Church the Feast of St. Joseph the Worker, May 1st.

I really want to make clear, William, how the Holy Spirit works through the Pope and Bishops of the Church. You must have noticed that, in my earlier letters, I used to say '(as the Church teaches)'. Such teaching is known as TRADITION (with a capital 'T'), and is the fulfilment of Christ's promise to the Apostles:

> '. . .when the spirit of truth comes, he will lead you to the complete truth' (Jn 16:13)

The Holy Spirit speaks now, **to and through** the Church, guiding her as He has ever done over the centuries.

Many serious matters that arise are responded to by a Synod (a gathering) of Bishops. When there has been a threat to the Faith, a heresy (i.e. a false teaching) to be dealt with – as has often been the case from the very beginning – it has been dealt with by a Council of the Church. The first, the Council of Jerusalem, *is in the Bible*. Important decisions were made there about the newly-converted Gentile (non-Jewish) Christians. (Read Acts 15 to get the whole picture. Note that the Apostles Peter and James speak. Authority!!)

This is hardly the time to give you an account of all the Councils of the Church, right up to the Second Vatican Council which took place some 30 years ago. I simply wished to say that this is the 'Apostle Peter' (the first Pope) steering the Church – sometimes called the 'barque of Peter' – as Simon Peter himself once steered his boat on the Sea of Galilee until he was called by the Lord to leave all and follow him.

I promise you my prayers in this time of trouble.

God bless you always!

Love, Auntie May

P.S. Don't forget to email me your questions! (And now, while I think of it, do you still have the same GP at home who treated you before? Or do you have to be at school when his surgery is open?)

Letter Three

11th Nov. St. Martin of Tours

Dear William,

I had your email. Yes, of course I understand you wrote that way because it's such a busy time. I may email you from time to time as well. We'll see.

Right! So Alicia is now living with her Gran and has found herself a job in a dress shop. You would like to go to Mass with the two of them at Christmas but haven't told them yet, and that is why you want me to tell you more about the Mass.

Before I start searching through my papers for something helpful I think I'd better mention some of the 'basics' of our behaviour in church. You will know from your experience in Montreal that there is a lot of sitting, standing and kneeling at different stages and it can seem rather overwhelming. We Catholics naturally take it for granted.

As we come through the church door we dip a finger in the 'holy water stoop' and make 'the sign of the cross' on ourselves, to remind us of our baptism and to acknowledge that we are entering the special presence of Jesus. Jesus is there, you see, in what is known as 'the tabernacle' – in the consecrated 'bread' known as the Blessed Sacrament – and before Alicia takes her seat you will see her genuflect (bend the knee), to acknowledge that Presence.

(If Gran's knees are as bad as you say, she may just bow her head). Just take your seat with them. They will look after you. I am hoping whatever attachment I manage to send with this letter will help you understand the reason for all this. We use our bodies to express what is in our hearts and minds. It will become easier as you grasp the meaning and get caught up in the worship.

Those present who are not Catholics are invited to come forward for a blessing at Communion time, but you may stay in your seat if you'd rather. How well I remember – while I was still having my instruction before being received into the Church – seeing my husband go forward for Communion, and wishing so much to be receiving Christ's Body and Blood as he did. Mind you, at Christmas, there will be many visitors not all of whom will be Catholic. Those children, too, who have not yet been prepared for First Holy Communion – which takes place annually in the early summer – will also go up to receive a blessing.

I should think Alicia and Gran will appreciate your coming with them at Christmas very much. I can't help thinking, however – special though Christmas is – it might be easier to be there on a more 'ordinary' day. Mind you, the Mass is the Mass, whether sung or said, whether celebrated in the presence of thousands or quietly with only a few.

I'll have to stop in a minute for Cuthbert's walk. That dog has a built-in timer, I'm sure! But I'd like to add a couple of things to this letter before working on what I like to call my attachment, although both will go in the post as usual!

You know I care about you, William, so I'm going ahead with one or two thoughts as to why you've had this flare up of your eczema. One of the worst things for anyone to cope with is someone else's ENVY. It shows itself as if that person were saying – and sometimes they do actually say – 'It's all very well for you!' It's not easy for the envious person to recognise that's what they are and so you can't challenge them. You are popular with the boys, young, and a newcomer. You also have a well-off father. This senior master may have struggled to get where he is. You get the picture?

A time of stress is likely to stir up memories of previous times, like that terrible time you and your dad were struggling with the loss of wife and mother. (You know already that I myself am no stranger to sudden loss.) And it made your dad even more 'anti-religion'. Maybe he still is, as he didn't want to go to church with you last Christmas? Let's – you and I – pray that the Lord will lead you safely to wherever he wants you to be, and calm your father's heart to stop 'blaming God' so he can peacefully let you follow your own path, and find his own.

Let's also pray for the master at your school.

Peace!

Love, Auntie May

ATTACHMENT 3B: MORE ABOUT THE MASS

We stand as the priest comes forward to the altar;

He says, 'In the name of the Father, the Son and the Holy Spirit' (all making the Sign of the Cross);

He then gives the Greeting, to which we respond as shown in the Missal (or in a booklet/sheet/card handed to you as you come into church).

And then: The priest leads us in acknowledging *our sinfulness.* We all say the Confiteor (I confess) together.

They did this in the early Church: *'On the Lord's own day, assemble in common to break bread and offer thanks, but first confess your sins, so that your sacrifice may be pure.'*[1]

The most ancient words follow (either in Greek). *Kyrie eleison - Christe eleison – Kyrie eleison* (or in English): *Lord have mercy – Christ have mercy – Lord have mercy*

The priest then says: 'May Almighty God have mercy on us, forgive us our sins, and bring us to everlasting life.' To which we reply: Amen.

---

[1] These words are found in a document called the Didache, from the early days of the Faith, almost certainly the First Century.

The Gloria (said or sung) follows – on Sundays and Feasts. You will find the whole Gloria in the Sunday Missal.

Next comes the Collect (The prayer for the day).

And then we sit for the Liturgy of the Word, which I already wrote about on Pentecost Sunday this year – in my 17th Letter.

LETTER FOUR

Dear William,

I am not surprised you recognised – in what I wrote about the Mass – a similar pattern of worship to what you have once or twice experienced in the Church of England.

I believe I should digress for a moment to explain the history of this. I tried to explain before that, what is now the 'Holy Communion Service' in that church, is basically what is still there after the changes made over the centuries since Henry VIII. You have an altar, a priest (though some would say 'a minister'), an acknowledgement of sins, a Collect, and Readings. There are also the commonly recognised seasons of the liturgical year like Christmas and Easter, and – in *some* of the churches – *some* of the Feasts.

Within the Church of England: as well as the differences in the style of worship between one church or parish and another, *there is some difference as to what is believed about the nature of the bread and wine at the time of Holy Communion.* Some believe Christ is truly present and High Church Anglican Priests perform virtually the same actions at the altar as Catholic Priests – that much I do know – but that came in through the 'Oxford Movement' after several centuries.

And Low Church parishes would not dream of following the beliefs and the style of worship High Church parishes engage in. Frankly, I get lost in all this – all within the established C of E. What the members certainly have in common is their Baptism, the Bible, an ordained ministry – not *assuredly* going back to the Apostles – and the Sovereign as their Head, which means the Queen chooses the bishops.

Sorry! I just got led astray into making comparisons, based on my own experience. I should remember that you only asked me to explain the Christian Faith as I know it now.

While, as I have told you already, the One, Holy, Catholic and Apostolic Church acknowledges as 'Christian' all who are baptised in the name of the Father, Son and Holy Spirit, she claims for herself the 'fullness' of the Faith.

You must go by your own experience, William.

Thinking about the beliefs of other Christians reminds me of something I asked you some time ago, and I've never had your answer. I invited you to guess how many different kinds of Protestant Christians there now are (all stemming from the split caused by the Reformation). Well? Like to email me a figure?

Now, about your other news, and mine. I gather you have to be at the school Monday morning to Friday evening and live in for one weekend in four for the sake of the boarders. I am so pleased you are able to be at home on the other weekends, and sometimes visit Alicia at her Gran's for Sunday tea. I suppose the dear girl is living there because of her job?

Things are much the same here. I am getting older (and so is Cuthbert). Likewise my car, which I rely on to get me to Mass and do my shopping in town. We did have a village shop when I first came here but that closed a few months ago. Going there used to be one of our daily walks in winter but now we walk past its closed windows, as far as the tiny school and then back home.

That's all for now.

Love, Auntie May

P.S. Keep praying, and don't let the criticism get to you!

ATTACHMENT 4B: THE MOVEMENTS OF THE MASS
After the Gospel (for which everyone stands) comes the Homily (where we sit).

We then stand to say (or sing) the Creed. In the Creed we are proclaiming our Faith, week by week (normally in English but at Christmas maybe in Latin!) and usually we do so using the Nicene Creed. This is the longer Creed of the two in regular use, and it proclaims in detail everything we believe.

Then (still standing) you will hear read 'The Prayers of the Faithful' (Bidding Prayers), written in and for that Parish each Sunday, with an emphasis on: the present needs of the whole Church; prayer for the Government (see I Timothy 2:2); and Parish needs (for example, those who have died or are sick).

Following a few moments of silent prayer, we all ask our Mother Mary to add her prayers to ours as we say together the prayer, *Hail Mary*.

THE OFFERTORY
On Sundays we sit for the Offertory Hymn, during which the collection bag or plate is passed round to receive our offering of money, but we stand while the Offertory gifts – the 'elements' of bread and wine – are brought to the altar from the back of the church, often by children. The priest, standing by the altar steps, receives these and passes them to an 'altar server' to be taken to the altar. (The collection is placed in front of the altar.)

The Offertory includes thanking God for the gifts – and all the ancient actions and words of priest and people in preparation for the Liturgy of the Eucharist, as follows:

THE SURSUM CORDA: 'LIFT UP YOUR HEARTS'
We stand for the ancient words inviting us to prepare for the Eucharist. The priest greets us and says, 'Lift up your hearts'. We agree it is right for us to give thanks and praise to God. The words – those *currently in use* (as determined by the

Magisterium for the whole Church) – will surely be there for you
to see and respond to, on the Mass Sheet or booklet.

THE PREFACE

The priest takes up our words as (standing behind the altar
and facing the people) he reads the Preface. This declares our
special reason for praising God on this particular Day, or in this
particular Season, and leads into the Sanctus. ('Holy, holy,
holy. . .') which on Christmas Day will almost certainly be
sung. Then we kneel for the priest to say the Eucharistic Prayer.
There are four such, to be used regularly for different occasions.
Eucharistic Prayer I (The Roman Canon) contains the names of
many Saints from the earliest days of the Church.

During this Prayer the bread and wine are consecrated – and so
become the Body and Blood of Christ – after which the priest
says: '*Let us proclaim the Mystery of Faith*' and all respond with
the Acclamation.

The Eucharistic Prayer then continues. . . . and concludes with:

'Through him, and with him, and in him,
O God, almighty Father,
In the unity of the Holy Spirit,
All glory and honour is yours,
For ever and ever.'

To which we say: *Amen*

THE COMMUNION RITE

We stand to say the Our Father together (pausing after the word 'evil' for the priest to add some words before we all come in again with:

'. . for the kingdom,
the power and the glory are yours,
now and for ever.')

THE PEACE

The priest says the prayer for peace and unity. He wishes us peace and we respond as given in the Missal. Then we are invited to 'exchange the sign of peace' by smiling at and shaking hands with those around us, and wishing them 'Peace.'

THE AGNUS DEI (still standing) *All say:*

'Lamb of God, who takes away the sins of the world,
have mercy on us.
'Lamb of God, who takes away the sins of the world,
have mercy on us.
'Lamb of God, who takes away the sins of the world,
grant us peace.'

The priest then raises the Host and the Chalice and says:

BEHOLD THE LAMB OF GOD.
BEHOLD HIM THAT TAKES AWAY
    THE SINS OF THE WORLD.
BLESSED ARE THOSE CALLED TO
    THE SUPPER OF THE LAMB.

All (kneeling) declare their unworthiness (in words recalling those of the centurion in the Bible): '*Lord, I am not worthy that you should enter under my roof.*'

The priest makes his Communion and then the people go forward in turn to receive. There may be a Communion Hymn.

THE CONCLUDING RITES (There may first be Notices.)
The priest again wishes the people 'PEACE' and we him. Then we stand for him to give us the BLESSING (which may include first a 'solemn' one for Christmas – in 3 parts with an Amen for each) and he sends us forth into the world. There should be a (rousing) final hymn / carol.

When Mass is over, some people, especially those with children, will go forward to look at the Crib. (An offering may be left there in a basket).

LETTER FIVE

Dear William,

After all this time, I have no idea when your birthday is! The reason I ask is that I was getting ready to send you a book for Christmas, but then thought perhaps it was not the right time. For one thing, it might get lost in the post. If your birthday turns out to be very much later on, I shall send you the book for Easter instead.

Needless to say, I hope everything goes well for you at Christmas and you enjoy the break from school. One advantage of the prep school system is that you get longer holidays. Being in the workshop may help give you a much-needed break. I do hope so. I expect your father will be there for Christmas itself and you will cook and eat together like last year. Are you able to invite Alicia to the house, I wonder? But maybe she needs to be with Gran at home whenever she is not at work. It's bound to be hectic in the shop with people buying presents and looking for new dresses to go out in. And she often has to do alterations, you said. A skilled young lady!

I'm attaching this time, something about the Blessed Sacrament – the bread that has become Christ's Body at the words of Our Lord spoken by the priest during the Eucharistic Prayer.

Yes, I am aware of doling out rather large helpings of information. It's just that I want to prepare you for going to Mass with
Alicia. As she is what we call 'a cradle Catholic', the Mass will
be like second nature to her. She may not sense how it might
come across to you.

Have a Happy Christmas, all of you!

I shall be at Mass of course, otherwise allowing Cuthbert to take
me for a walk or re-reading some of the books so neatly arranged
on those beautiful oak shelves. Thanks again!

Love, Auntie May

5B THE BLESSED SACRAMENT; AND A WORD ABOUT CHRISTMAS DAY

Let nothing take from you the JOY and PEACE that come from
worshipping 'the new-born King'!!

We come to Mass that day as always:

to praise God together in his Presence;

to hear him speak in the Scriptures;

to offer our gifts and ourselves in thanksgiving;

to participate in the Sacrifice of the Mass, as we see and

hear the priest carry out Jesus' command;

to eat Christ's Body and drink his Blood,

to express, in the Our Father, our desire for the Kingdom

to receive God's Blessing and

then to go forth to do his Will in our lives.

After Communion the priest takes any remaining consecrated hosts to the Tabernacle, to be kept there for the sick at home, or to be brought to the altar during the next Communion time if extra Hosts are needed. I once heard a young child say, 'There's Father putting Jesus away in the cupboard.'!! How true! Jesus is in the Blessed Sacrament.

In the tabernacle there will also be a large Host, sometimes transferred to a beautiful gold 'monstrance' and placed on the altar for a time of 'Eucharistic Adoration' or 'Adoration of the Blessed Sacrament'. This can be simply a period of silence or a Holy Hour with hymns and readings at intervals, ending with Benediction. (Benediction I shall explain later.)

It is Jesus' Presence we acknowledge as we genuflect on entering the church. If he is present on the altar we go down on both knees. This Presence is what makes a Catholic Church feel peaceful. (I truly believe you felt it at St. Mark's in Venice.)

A word about the date of Christmas. As far as we know, 25th December did not appear as the Birthday of Christ until 336 AD. It replaced a pagan festival. Earlier the important Feasts were Epiphany and Easter. A consequence of the change is that Christmas Day finds itself followed immediately by Saints'

Days that were already on the calendar before: namely St. Stephen, St. John the Evangelist, and the Holy Innocents.

May the joy of Christmas be always in our hearts!

LETTER SIX

The Holy Family

Dear William,

What a Christmas it was for you! I hardly know where to start. With your father, I think. I was truly sorry to hear about his fall and his broken arm.

Not a good way to begin a New Year, but a blessing in disguise, seeing that Alicia has now been round to your place more than once and charmed him with her smile – and her cooking!

That will have made up for his anger at your plan to go to Mass at Christmas. Ah well, we must forgive him. It all goes to show that 'God can write straight on crooked lines' as a friend of mine, Sister Madeleine, used to say. (She was from Canada, incidentally.)

From what you've recently told me, I now realise Alicia's Gran is actually her great grandmother, and much older than I had been thinking. 'Gran' was what she was to Alicia's mum. Alicia's own grandmother, must be 'Nan' I suppose? And it turns out that, for Gran's sake, the three of you went to the 'Mass during the Day' at 10.30, while I was imagining you there at midnight.

Anyway, it sounds as if you had the lunch well organised for the two of you at home, and your father mellowed a little after that. Her family will have missed Alicia at Christmas, no doubt, but her sisters and brothers will have rallied round. Are they all younger?

You've said very little about the 'adventure' of going to Mass (in English this time), but made a point of telling me about the little children visiting the Crib, and that it did remind you of your own feelings when you were that age. I'm so glad.

I think, William, we always miss our mothers, whatever age we are when the Lord takes them. Seven was such a young age for so great a loss. I was nineteen when mine died. I hope your two friends – young and not-so-young – were some help in overcoming the sad memories. Could this be the start of something new?

That reminds me to ask after Martin and Richard and their family. They were very good to you. Are you still in touch?

I'll be relieved when this winter is over. It's been very cold, and icy on the roads. I always walk with a stick at this time of the year . . .and ask St. Michael the Archangel and my Guardian Angel to watch over me. Sometimes my neighbour calls to say he's going out with his two dogs and would Cuthbert like to join them. So kind!

That's quite enough for now. I've a lot of stuff to pass on in my extra page.

Happy New Year to you, your father, and your friends!

Love from, Auntie May

6B COMMENTS ON THE HOLY FAMILY AND ON THE ROSARY

Isn't it wonderful that God the Father arranged a family for his Son!

Mary, the Mother chosen before time began, needed the guardianship of a husband, St. Joseph; and Jesus, in his humanity, had to grow from a newborn infant to full adulthood, learning all the time (Luke 2:52).

On this Feast, which takes place on the Sunday within the Octave of Christmas, the focus is on the family and this is reflected in the Readings of our current Missal:

Year A: Ecclesiasticus 3:2-6, 12-14; Psalm 127:1-5; Colossians 3:12-21; Mt 2:13-15.19-23.

Year B: Genesis 15:1-6. 21:1-3; Psalm 32:4-6, 9, 18-20; Hebrews11:8.11-12.17-19; Luke 2:22-40.

Year C: Samuel I:20-22, 24-28; Psalm 83:2-3,5-6,9-10. I John 3:1-2.21-24; Luke 2:41-52.

The family is the all-important unit in the Church. It is in the family that children are to be cared for, nurtured and taught. Jesus said, '*See that you never despise any of these little ones, for I tell you that their angels are continually in the presence of my Father in heaven*'. (Mt 18:10) (See also Mt 18:6 and Mark 9:42.)

The breakdown of family life is one of the saddest developments in the modern world. The wars, the increase in unbelief and the consequent lowering of standards of morality have all added to the 'mess' our society is in.

THE ROSARY

I am inclined to think that only those who say the Rosary often can realise the value of it. It is misunderstood by 'those outside' because it sounds repetitive. There is a saying, however, that: *'The family that prays together, stays together'*. I envy my friends who grew up in such families. They do have a strong bond. What converts will hopefully learn to appreciate – and outsiders often do not comprehend – is that the Rosary is not intended to be merely a set of prayers to be said. For each 'decade' (of one Our Father, ten Hail Marys, and one Glory be) there is a 'mystery' to be pondered upon, over and above the prayers we are reciting and the passing of our fingers over the beads.

The Rosary allows for five decades each time to complete the circle. Each set of five has its own 'Mysteries' calling us to meditate on aspects of the life of Our Lord, and also of his Mother, 'Our Lady'.

To start with – and especially for the Feast of the Holy Family – we have:

THE JOYFUL MYSTERIES
The Annunciation *(as in Luke 1:26-38)*
The Visitation *(Luke 1:39-56)*
The Nativity *(Luke 2:1-19)*

The Presentation of the Infant Jesus in the Temple *(Luke 2:22-38)*
The Child Jesus remaining behind in the Temple *(Luke 2:41-50)*

Family / group members take it in turns to lead a decade.
And at the end of the whole we say:

V. *Pray for us O Holy Mother of God.*
R. *That we may be made worthy of the promises of Christ.*

Then the prayer (*Salve regina*):
'*Hail, Holy Queen, Mother of Mercy. . .'*

And, to finish: '*O God, whose Only-begotten Son, by his Life, Death
and Resurrection, has purchased for us the rewards of Eternal Life,
grant that meditating upon the sacred Mysteries of the most holy
Rosary of the Blessed Virgin Mary, we may both imitate what they
contain and obtain what they promise. Through Christ Our Lord.
Amen'*

There are several other prayers that are frequently added. . .
including '*St. Joseph, Pray for us'*. Friends of mine in Ireland used
to follow with a Litany, and finish with '*Thanks be to God for that
much said.'*!!

LETTER SEVEN

Dear William,

It's a late Easter this year. Crocuses are already brightening my tiny patch of garden, and a few daffodils nearest the house have dared to poke their heads several inches above ground. It's better if they don't bloom, though, until the March winds have died.

Lots of rain, but I do have some central heating as well as the log fire, so Cuthbert and I can dry ourselves off between one walk and the next. (I have two coats and he has only one, but he has several old towels to rub himself down with – except he leaves that to me!)

Today I went to Mass and came out with a smudge of ashes on my forehead. We are given that mark either with the words, 'Turn away from sin and be faithful to the Gospel' or 'Remember, man, you are dust and to dust you will return'. Yes, we are expected to fast, for reasons that I'll say more about in a moment. Some monastic Orders fast every Wednesday and Friday. Certain Saints have also fasted on those days throughout the year. Again, more on that in a moment.

I have to remind myself from time to time that I am not just here to tell you about the Catholic Faith. I know you consider me your friend, and the same is true for me. So, as a friend, I'd like to pass on some wisdom about two things.

One is the supreme importance of PRAYER. I mean by that a daily (hourly) walking with, and talking to, – and above all, listening to – the God in whose name you were baptised.

Didn't Jesus say he would be with us always?
Didn't he give us the Holy Spirit?

For someone like yourself, who had no follow-up – of teaching or encouragement, or help in getting to know Jesus personally – what matters is to understand that the GRACE of your Baptism is *indelible*. It is a mark of belonging that cannot be 'rubbed out'.

It is by God's Grace that you started seeking the TRUTH – about the History you were being taught, and what you were hearing from your Christian friends. At his trial before Pontius Pilate, Jesus said: '*I was born for this, I came into the world for this, to bear witness to the truth; and all who are on the side of truth listen to my voice.*'

This gradual 'coming alive' of a person baptised as a baby, is something I think of as I hold in my hand the bulbs I am about to plant in autumn, and think of the daffodils and tulips that will come up in the spring.

Bulbs and seeds – especially the seeds of the great trees, William

– have to go through the cold of winter as well as the warmth of summer. This is a sort of 'parable' of our lives, too. Sorrows and difficulties of every kind are sent to aid our growth (see Mt 16:24; Mk 8:34; Lk 9:23). Likewise the grace to deal with them!

I'm glad you've told me quite how difficult this term is proving. I can only repeat that you will need to ask for the grace of FORGIVENESS. It is an act of the will, not a feeling. There it is – right there in the Our Father! And I'll give you a tip. It becomes easier if you can somehow find a reason to *excuse*. Is there any way you can work around to feeling sorry for the master who is picking on you? And for the (probably very lonely) little boy who started the rumour that 'Sir might have leprosy'?

We are all in need of forgiveness. It's that way round in the prayer as well. We actually have to forgive before we can be forgiven. And one more thing. When Our Lord wished to forgive those who nailed him to his Cross, he said, '*Father, forgive them.*' And his reason? '*. . .they do not know what they are doing.*' '*Love your enemies*' by praying a blessing on them and it will begin to ease your pain at their treatment of you.

I should have said earlier. . . what a blessing that – through her friends at work – Alicia found someone to help your father manage while he still has his arm in plaster. You say he's growing quite fond of that dear girl of yours, even though she's a Catholic!! (Well?)

Anyway. . .as you are planning to go to Mass again during

the Easter break I have decided to send you a Missal for your birthday, as originally planned. But as that is so soon, the parcel may not get there in time. When I rang to order they told me a reprint is due, so we must hope there are still copies to hand.

My love to you as always,

Auntie May

7B THE MEANING OF LENT

Lent is a word meaning 'Spring'. It was a time of food shortages after the winter stocks had been used up. But for Christians it is a time of:

recalling Jesus' days in the wilderness, following his Baptism.

repenting of our sins and resolving to 'pull our socks up' and start leading a less worldly and more holy life.

preparing to follow Jesus through the days of his great saving act (our Redemption) during Holy Week and Easter.

For some, known as catechumens – those who are getting ready to be baptised as adults – there are special prayers to mark their last few steps towards the Easter Vigil, when they will be welcomed into the Church.

So . . . giving up chocolate? Well, yes, if chocolate (or cake? or beer?) is your weakness. This can be done as a discipline and a reminder that we do not depend on material things for our salvation. It is good to include putting by the money we would have spent on those things, and giving it away to someone in need. 'Almsgiving' that is called. We should do it secretly, Jesus said. There is a lot about the value of almsgiving in the Book of Tobit. (Sorry! That book isn't in your *Good News Bible*.)

Lent is also when we should give extra time to prayer. Some people get up half-an-hour earlier to spend time in silence or reading the Scriptures. We fast on Ash Wednesday and on Good Friday. As far back as the *Didache* the advice was given to fast on Wednesdays and Fridays (and some do it all year, not only those in monasteries and convents, but also ordinary lay people like us). The reason given in those early days, however, was that pagans fasted on Mondays and Tuesdays!

Let us take just one example of the Scripture readings for a Sunday in Lent: the Second Sunday (Year B).

Genesis 27:1-2, 9-13,15-18: Abraham, our father in faith, preparing to sacrifice his son, Isaac, (a 'type' of the Father sacrificing his only Son, Jesus)

verses from Psalm 115, with the Response: '*I will walk in the presence of the Lord in the land of the living*'.

Romans 8: 31-34 '*God did not spare his own Son*'.

And the Gospel is Mark's account of the Transfiguration, (9:2-10), an event which has its own Feast in August as well.

OUR NEED FOR REDEMPTION
The big question is: **Why did Jesus need to come and save us?** Here's how I summarised it in one of my essays. . .

CREATION, FALL AND PROMISE
'In the beginning' (Gen 1:1), God, saying, *'Let us make man in our own image'* (Gen 1:26), created the first man and woman (v.27) and set them in a paradise garden, to be masters of the rest of Creation and to freely love and obey him, receiving everything from his hand. But then came 'the Fall' (Gen 3:1-7)! These two disobeyed, succumbing to temptation and thereby bequeathing to us, their descendants, the same tendency, known as 'original sin'. They hid from God! They forfeited their earthly paradise. Their vision of God was no longer clear. They stood in need of a Redeemer.

Then God gave an initial 'sign', a promise of redemption to come (Gen 3:15); and there followed a centuries-long process by which God as it were 're-revealed' and then 'further revealed' himself to fallen humanity.

Note: We – humanity that is – really did finish up better off even than we could have been had Adam not sinned. We find this expressed in the *Exsultet* which is sung – usually by a Deacon, if there is one – at the first great Mass of Easter, the Easter Vigil. There we find the words:

'O happy fault, O necessary sin of Adam,
Which gained for us so great a Redeemer!'

May our Lent be well spent and our hearts made ready!

Letter Eight

Dear William,

Well now. . . that's a hard decision. This is your first job and it's a big step to give it up after one year. But, if I've understood you correctly, you are not doing it because of your troubles but for another reason. . .so that you can spend a whole year with Uncle Jack and learn more about what it takes to earn your living full-time in the carpentry trade.

One question. Have you not enjoyed teaching your 8 year olds?

Yes, I do know you have to give a whole term's notice, and so before the Easter holidays. It can be tricky. I have been in that position myself. At least it will be summer, with more time spent outdoors on the playing fields or on what we used to call 'nature walks'. I do so love the summer, with the long days and the trees all in full leaf. Only the flies are a bother. (Cuthbert is nodding.)

Today's Feast is, of course, most special for Wales. March also hosts the Patron Saint of Ireland, St. Patrick. We get our turn in April with St. George. I suppose it's good to be patriotic, but these Saints – with their example and their prayers – do belong to the whole Church nevertheless.

That reminds me to say that the Novena to St. Joseph begins on March 10th. He is, of course, happy to intercede for the whole world, but you are about to share in an experience of work on earth that is like his own and he will surely be close to you.

Six days after St. Joseph's Day we have the precious Solemnity of the Annunciation of the Lord. What a beautiful day! We are told, that heaven and earth were waiting for Mary's 'Yes' so that the Son of God could become Man and perfectly reveal the Father.

You've not said whether you are still in touch with Martin and Richard. I sometimes ask myself whether you miss the Christian groups you used to attend together. But you've already said you intend to go to church with Alicia at Easter, and so I am carrying on with my words about the Catholic Faith.

Love from your Auntie May.

8B PREPARING FOR EASTER: THE SACRAMENT OF RECONCILIATION

After so much about Holy Days, it is important to stress that Lent is about every day. In fact the whole of life is about *every day*. Jesus told us this (Mt 6:34)

We, as individuals, have prayer and almsgiving – and abstinence (the 'giving up chocolate' bit) to offer. All of this should be secret between ourselves and our Father in heaven.

But the Church as a whole also gives up certain things during the Lenten Season. There are no Alleluias; no GLORIA, even at Sunday Mass; and no flowers in the Sanctuary.

The Church also provides for the confession of sins in the Sacrament of Reconciliation. It is available all year but with the Lenten emphasis on repentance, we Catholics are especially encouraged to come and 'make our confession' to the priest as part of our preparation for Easter. This is done privately, in the 'confessional' which is part of the church building.

I can almost hear the Protestants 'protesting'! They will tell you that sins are to be confessed to God alone. What I have learned, however, is that there is more than one purpose to this Sacrament. There is the promised SECRECY. When St. James wrote *'confess your sins to one another'* (James 5:16), he could not have known that the people would fail to keep secret what they heard. What many non-Catholics also do not know is that the priest represents not only Christ but also our fellow-Christians, against whom – as well as against God – we have sinned because we are all one body in Christ.

As 'a penitent' we are usually given some ADVICE after we have confessed, and then a PENANCE –most often a prayer to say or some Scripture to read – as a mark of our sorrow at having offended God and to 'make up for' having wounded Christ's Body the Church.

We then make an ACT OF CONTRITION, words that speak of our

sorrow at having offended God by sinning, and 'a firm purpose of amendment' – meaning our promise to avoid sin in future.

Finally the priest – acting in persona Christi – will give the penitent ABSOLUTION *in the Name of Father, and of the Son and of the Holy Spirit.*

LETTER NINE

Dear William,

It is good to know that you will be back at home by next weekend – by the evening of your birthday, in fact. I'll be posting your
card and the Missal on Monday to make quite sure they reach
you in time.

March will be over by the middle of the week and I'm glad to
say the daffodils are not all blown over. There will be the scent
of narcissi and lilies in church on Easter Day. I do so love that!

I'm wondering how the Head will react to your resignation. But
really it scarcely matters – except, of course, for needing a refer-
ence for any future post as a teacher. You sound very certain that
you want spend your life among shavings and sawdust, but
who knows? Life can take strange turns.

Please remember me to your Catholic friends. I'm guessing – in
fact I'd even bet on it (though not literally, as my Quaker
upbringing did not allow gambling) that Gran and Alicia say
the Rosary each evening. I have fond memories of being in
Ireland and joining in with the prayers at five o'clock. I'll say
something more on the subject of the Mysteries in the second
part of this letter.

(I think of it as the 'attachment' but can't get out of the habit of posting things in a letter box. Ours is in a wall and has the initials VR. I wonder when in Queen Victoria's long reign it first appeared?)

Speaking of that century reminds me that we never got back to the topic of what was happening to Catholics in those days. Up to 1829 a Catholic could not vote or be a Member of Parliament, and could not inherit property – or so I've heard. What a danger they were to the nation!

Thinking of property reminds me to ask how your father is coping with his house and large garden. I suppose you will be busy in the garden again soon. But what will happen when you are away for so long in Canada? Forgive me. I'm just so full of questions.

I'm looking forward to Holy Week and Easter, and hoping for sunnier weather in the weeks beyond.

Love, Auntie May

9B CHRIST'S SUFFERING AND OUR OWN.
THE SORROWFUL MYSTERIES

From the hymn writer, Mrs Alexander, we have this verse (see the hymn that begins *There is a green hill far away*):

'We may not know, we cannot tell
What pains he had to bear,
But we believe it was for us
He hung and suffered there.'

You'll agree, I am sure, that this is a child's way of looking at the Passion and Death of Our Lord, yet it goes to the heart of it.

As Catholics we are taught that the sufferings of Christ are to be pondered by us in the context of the Eucharist. This puts the emphasis on thanksgiving – which is the meaning of the word 'eucharist' – and can lead us to an adult understanding of how Christ's Sacrifice on the Cross began with his gift of his Body and Blood to the Apostles the night before.

Hear the words of St. Peter:

For you know that the price of your ransom. . .was paid, not in
anything perishable like silver or gold, but in precious blood as
of a blameless and spotless lamb, Christ. (I Peter 1:18-19)

Because the Church teaches that the very substance of the elements of bread and wine offered at the Mass – as the priest says the words of Christ – is totally transformed into the Body and Blood of Christ, this means we have before us Christ's Sacrifice for our salvation.

One of the great gifts of the Catholic Church to its members – and I have heard two converts agreeing with each other on the special value of this – is the knowledge that we can draw close to Christ's suffering and can unite our suffering with his for the benefit of the Church and for the conversion of the world.

Hear the words of St. Paul:

> *I have been crucified with Christ, and yet I am alive; yet it is no longer I, but Christ living in me.' (Galatians 2:20) 'It makes me happy to be suffering for you now, and in my own body to make up all the hardships that still have to be undergone by Christ for the sake of his body, the Church. . .'* (Colossians 1:24)

This attitude to suffering makes it *redemptive*. Although we may be wishing to say, 'OUCH!' at what is happening to us, we simply have to remember what we are often told: 'OFFER IT UP!' and soon we are aware of Jesus' words:

> *Come unto me* . . . (Matthew 11:28-29)

Yet to get some conception of Christ's Passion – in an adult way – we have been given the SORROWFUL Mysteries of the Holy

Rosary:

> **The Agony in the Garden** (Luke 22:44)
> **The Scourging at the Pillar** (John 19:1)
> **The Crown of Thorns** (Matthew 27:29)
> **The Way to Calvary** (John 19:18)
> **The Crucifixion** (Luke 23:46)

These take their turn after the Joyful Mysteries, and are followed by the Glorious Mysteries.

Some say all three each day, but more often the Joyful are said on Mondays, Thursdays and Saturdays; the Sorrowful on Tuesdays and Fridays; and the Glorious on Wednesdays and Sundays.

May God bless your Holy Week and give you heartfelt rejoicing on the Day of Resurrection!

LETTER TEN

Dear William,

Thanks for letting me know the parcel was waiting for you when you got home. I thought it high time you could see for yourself how the Church celebrates the very many important times in each Liturgical Year, but especially Easter.

I'm certain Alicia will have understood that Dad wanted you at home for the remainder of your birthday. But it was nice you took her out the next evening.

And now . . .what astonishing news! So Martin is to be married in July and you are invited to the wedding. Well, well! Did he send a photo of his fiancée? (Of course I'm nosy! Why not?)

And then there is all your other news, about the holiday and about your father. Let's take that last item first. So, after all these years he has met a new woman. I suppose he feels you are sorting out your own life. Maybe he even felt lonely at the thought of you away for so long. I will pray his new friendship is part of God's plan. Have you met her? How is his arm, by the way?

Meanwhile, you have been grateful to have time with Alicia, despite working hard to put the garden straight.

On a deeper level, thank you for sharing with me how you felt about going to Mass all through this all-important season. Yes, I do realise it was partly 'to give an arm to Gran who is finding it more difficult to get around now'. And I'm sorry Alicia had trouble getting time off on Good Friday. It is a Bank Holiday, after all!

But that was a special day for you and I note that you felt the difference it makes when the tabernacle is empty. It gives us a sense of how bereft the disciples must have felt during that Sabbath when they had left the dear Lord in the tomb!

And then the JOY OF THE RESURRECTION! How special it seems when you have followed Jesus so closely on the path through his Passion, Death and Burial.

I love to read what are called the 'Resurrection appearances', most especially John 21, starting with Peter suggesting a night of fishing – unsuccessful until Jesus gave them the command! And then, can you believe it? He, the Risen Lord, cooked break-fast!!

Some years ago I read a book by Fr Ian Petit OSB, *The God Who Speaks*, in which he said that Christ triumphed over death '...and we get through hanging on to his shirt tails.' Delightful way of putting it! Some words that the priest says during the Offertory tell us that as Jesus shares in our humanity so he invites us to share in his divinity.

We are adopted children of God! We just have to learn to live like it. This we do with the help of his grace, which makes it possible to avoid temptation, love God and our neighbour, and trust God for all our needs. Praise and thanksgiving are God's due, William, and it is right to give thanks and praise at all times – even when we don't feel like it.

I hope you get on well this term. Glad you can get out and coach cricket.

Send me an email any time. I suppose that is how we shall be keeping in touch when you are abroad. Meanwhile, I'm planning the second half of this letter – the tenth since we started writing again last November – and hoping it will reach you very soon.

Oh yes! Please reassure Alicia that I love Cuthbert very much and my remarks about him are not meant to be unkind. He's getting very stiff in his old age, you know. I'm wondering if his legs will carry him as far as the reservoir this year. We usually picnic there and watch the waterfowl.

Another two months and the swallows may be here, heralding summer.

Love, Auntie May

P.S. Tomorrow's Saint is St. Anselm (1033-1109 A.D.) who was Archbishop of Canterbury. A difficult time to be an archbishop in England.

10B THE GLORIOUS MYSTERIES AND THE VIRGIN MARY

These Mysteries are about our salvation and hope of eternal life.

The Resurrection of Our Lord Jesus Christ (Mark 16.7)
His Ascension to Heaven (Mark 16.19)
The Descent of the Holy Spirit at Pentecost (Acts 2:4)
The Assumption of Our Lady (John 14.3)
Our Lady crowned Queen of Heaven (Revelation 12.1)

The first three are quite clear but there are likely to be questions about the final two from anyone not brought up in the Church. And so there are several aspects of these Mysteries to consider.

The Scriptures tell us that Mary was 'full of grace' when the Angel Gabriel came to her at the Annunciation. The Church gradually came to understand that she was *full of grace* from the moment of her conception. (The Immaculate Conception was pronounced dogma by Pope Pius IX in 1854.) Also, as Scripture indicates, Jesus has promised to bring to Heaven those for whom he has *'prepare(d) a place'*. St. Paul also says that Jesus will raise from death *'all. . .in their proper order'* (I Corinthians 15:22).

There is no known grave of Mary, and she was long believed to have been assumed body and soul into heaven after her death, which is sometimes referred to as her 'Dormition' or 'Falling Asleep'. Belief in her Assumption was around for many centuries – as witnessed by paintings – but was not declared dogma until 1950 on All Saints Day by Pope Pius XII. Her Crowning in Heaven follows as a matter of course – supported by Revelation 12:1 – and has been confirmed over the centuries by her apparitions – particularly at Fatima in 1917.

Jesus said that the Spirit would lead the Church into all truth (Jn 16:13-15). He did not say that from the Day of Pentecost the Apostles would immediately understand everything!! You see, the world needed first to learn Christ as its Saviour; to understand him as God and Man; and the One God as Father, Son and Holy Spirit, the Trinity.

And, just as it took seven Ecumenical Councils to 'unwrap' everything that is to be believed about the Trinity who is God, so what is true of the Blessed Virgin also had to wait its turn.

Catholics do not *worship* Mary. She is a *creature*.

The Church honours her, and in doing so, honours God.

LETTER ELEVEN

June 1st. St. Justin Martyr

Dear William,

What wonderful weather we are having! I'm glad for you as it makes the cricket season so much easier to manage. And fancy that small boy turning into such a super fielder! You never told me his name but I have always thought of him as 'Bates-Jones', don't ask me why.

There's not a great deal of news from my neck of the woods. Last month's rain gave me extra work in the garden. Why do the weeds grow at twice the rate of the vegetables?

We may be having a new parish priest at my church by next year. Dear Father John is due for retirement next summer, as he is nearly 75.

I'm waiting to hear more about Martin's wedding. Of course I'm really surprised that he is not marrying in his own home church. You say his bride-to-be has not been attending his church for long and her parents want a traditional Church of England ceremony at St. James's, with the photos in the paper and the reception in a hotel. I wonder how Martin's family feels about it, and most especially Richard who is best man. July 22nd, I think you said.

After the end of term. I'll be interested to know how it all goes. Will you be able to stay with them, William, or will you have to find your own accommodation?

Now, back to our own topic!

You say you'd like to know what written authority lies behind my constant reminders of the Church's teachings, which you hear me speak of as TRADITION.

Tradition is the voice of the God-given Authority of the Pope and bishops who can claim Apostolic Succession. We hear it from the earliest Saints, of which today's Saint (St. Justin) is one – martyred around 165 A.D.

Of course, the Church relies on Scripture, far more than some Protestants appear to think. But it is always Scripture and Tradition, NOT 'Scripture alone'. I do not mean to be unkind, but I sometimes want to point out that the Bible did not exactly drop down from heaven! Nor did each Apostle receive a signed copy from Jesus himself!!

No, the truth is that Jesus gave us the Church and it was the Church, under the guidance of the Holy Spirit, that finally decided which books should make up the 'canon' of Scripture, both Old and New Testaments. When? Well, not until the Council of Carthage in 397 A.D.!

The book I am about to send you is not an ancient book, but

contains the accumulated wisdom of the Church over the centuries. This copy was published in 1994 under the guidance of our present Pope, and includes the wisdom of the Second Vatican Council, which ended in 1965.

I'll leave it there, I think, and write separately about the book, **The Catechism of the Catholic Church**, in my follow-up page. God bless you, William, in all that he sends!

Love, Auntie May

11B THE CATECHISM OF THE CATHOLIC CHURCH (CCC)
This is a volume that can tell you everything you need to know about the beliefs and teachings of the One, Holy, Catholic and Apostolic Church.

What is more, it is easy to read – well referenced and cross-referenced – and at the end of each section there is a box headed 'In Brief' which summarises what has just been explained.

There are several things to note:

The Prologue (p.7) is not to be missed. It is very clear and explains how everything is laid out – also who it is that can benefit from using the Catechism. Basically, everyone!!

PART ONE:
a) deals with how we come to believe; our capacity for God; and how he reveals himself to us.

b) next comes a clear and comprehensive statement of the Church's dependence on Sacred Scripture and the Holy Spirit as its interpreter. Then a description of the Canon of Scripture (P.32), followed by a statement as to the power of Scripture in the life of the Church.

c) MAN'S RESPONSE TO GOD. A summary on 'The Obedience of Faith' is followed by a complete 'run-through' of the CREED. PART TWO deals with CELEBRATION OF THE CHRISTIAN MYSTERY. It covers the Seven Sacraments.

PART THREE is about LIFE IN CHRIST. It covers our vocation, which is 'Life in the Spirit'. Notice how the Church is our interpreter and guide (Pp.442-3). a) The BEATITUDES. b) a long section on the TEN COMMANDMENTS. These form the basis of our moral lives.

Finally, SECTION IV is on PRAYER. The Subject Index not only shows you where to find the topics, but incidentally shows the importance of each – revealed by the amount of attention given to it.

LETTER TWELVE

Dear William,

At one time you might have been forgiven for thinking St. Cuthbert was an 'early' Saint. Well so he was, in England. But as I hope I showed you through St. Justin, there were Saints in Europe in the second century – and indeed in the first! How could the Gospel writers not be in heaven?

What matters for the Church is that we still have some of the writings of these 'early Fathers' as they are so often called. You will find many of them referred to in the footnotes of the Catechism. They are our witnesses to the Church's roots in 'apostolic times'.

At the point where St. Cyril of Alexandria appeared on the scene, the Church was fighting the heresy of the Nestorians, and he had a great deal to do with that. The Nestorians held that in Christ were two persons, one human and one divine. The Church, however, came to understand – through the Holy Spirit who leads the Church into all truth – that Christ is one Person with two natures. This is called 'the hypostatic union' and is in keeping with belief in the Trinity.

I'm talking now about the Council of Ephesus in AD 431 – the time when the Blessed Virgin Mary, Mother of Christ, was understood to be *theotokos*, 'Mother of God'.

Well now, I'm quite sure I can safely leave the Catechism to explain everything you need to know!! Although I'm hoping we may still have some interesting discussions in future, especially if you meet with further challenges from Protestants. That was where we started, wasn't it?

Just a couple of weeks to the end of term, I believe you said. The exams have finished and I suppose the reports are to be written. I fully expect to hear that you are sad at leaving, even though you have no doubts. Every place in which we spend time becomes familiar and 'tugs' at us when it's time to move on.

With love, Auntie May

LETTER THIRTEEN

June 28th Eve of the Solemnity of SS. Peter and Paul, Apostles

Dear William,

I posted my last letter only yesterday and yours arrived today but I felt it should have an immediate answer.

So Alicia is to be a bridesmaid! You say it is to be a Catholic wedding but she did not meet the couple at church. Instead she was asked at work to help the bride-to-be choose something to wear, and alter the dress as needed. Well, I'm sure that Alicia will use her excellent dressmaking skills to produce something beautiful for Anne – and for herself as bridesmaid!

When and where is the wedding to take place? At Sacred Heart church? Will you be there, do you think?

I remember well that my first husband asked me to marry him in the Catholic church and we had a Nuptial Mass. It meant that, as I was still an Anglican, we knelt together at the time for Communion (people knelt in those days) but he could receive and I could not.

It was still a happy occasion, of course. I've already told you that it was harder at our second Christmas when I was by then preparing to come into the Church. There was I, thinking that we would have many years – many Christmases – together in the future and never dreaming that he would be taken from me so soon. We do right to pray, *'Thy will be done'*. Jesus told us his followers must *'take up* (their) *cross daily'*.

There is unity in a Catholic marriage, William. And it is permanent– no divorce! So it is not to be undertaken lightly. There is generally a period of preparation/teaching beforehand. Today's solemnity is also very special. How much we all, as Christians, owe to these two great Saints – 'pillars of the Church'! Peter: with Jesus, of course, from the early days of the 'preaching of the Kingdom'; inspired by God to recognise Jesus as the Messiah; and therefore renamed 'the Rock' and chosen leader of the Apostles – the first Pope. Then Saul, also named Paul: a strict Pharisee (though also by birth a Roman citizen); an ardent persecutor of the first followers of the Risen Jesus; but suddenly called by that same Risen Jesus to become a follower himself, and counted among the Apostles because Christ himself had appointed and sent him to bring the Good News to the Gentile world.

Those letters, William! How poor we would be without them! They were in circulation in the earliest Church, before and after the Gospels were written, and were followed by others from the leaders (bishops), among them St. Ignatius of Antioch who had known – and had been baptised by – the Apostle John himself! (More of this another time.)

I must stop now as Cuthbert's time-clock is making him look up at his lead hanging on a peg near the door. At least it's a dry day! I'll write again soon while you are still in this country.

Love from, Auntie May

Letter Fourteen

Dear William,

I see! Well, I shall respect Alicia's confidence, of course. (I am even writing this by hand so there will be no record on my computer.)

It was clever of the dear girl to use the idea she had read about in the life of Maria von Trapp (of 'The Sound of Music' fame). So the bride-to-be's dress had to make her look bigger above the waist, to match her girth further down –then no-one would know she was expecting!!

You say the wedding was last week, before you got home, and was a very quiet ceremony anyway, but Alicia has shown you some photos of herself as bridesmaid, 'looking slim and lovely in a pale blue dress and holding pink roses.' Charming!

You know, William, it never ceases to amaze me that Catholic couples, who have been baptised and later confirmed – in my opinion, sometimes rather too young – go on to choose to 'live together' outside marriage.

Yes, I know. 'Everyone' is doing it! The forces of evil have made sure it is seen as a sort of 'practice run' and 'much better than a marriage breakdown followed by divorce'.

But in the eyes of God and his Church it is a 'mortal sin' and those who 'cohabit' (the official term) are putting their souls at risk! I should add that – as a sign – they are not permitted to receive the Body and Blood of Christ at Mass!

(By the way, the Sacrament of Reconciliation is compulsory, you should know, for anyone in mortal sin.)

Well, thank God, these two have seen sense, come back to the Faith, and are now husband and wife. So hopefully the child will be baptised, and grow up in a family. Praise God!

I shall pray for them.

Meanwhile I am looking forward to hearing about that other wedding – Martin's! When you write about it – as I sincerely hope you will – please don't forget to let me know the bride's name.

Love, Auntie May.

LETTER FIFTEEN

August 1st St. Alphonsus Liguori, Bishop and Doctor

Dear William,

Thank you for your long letter about Martin's wedding. Yes, as you say, Church of England weddings are kind of familiar to us and feel like 'the norm'. I trust Martin and Catherine will have a long and happy life together!

But I still imagine it must have seemed strange to your friend and his family, who would naturally have expected the wedding to take place in their own church with their own pastor and their own congregation.

Well, dear William, you'll be gone in a few days and, knowing that Uncle Jack will keep you very busy, I shan't expect anything like the number of letters I've been getting from you since we started writing – more than two years ago now!

I'll simply invite you to email me or write when there is any special news.

I expect you will keep in touch with Alicia and Gran, as well as your dad, naturally. Please let me have their news as well. I can't help caring about you all, you see. You are all in my prayers.

Even Cuthbert would miss hearing your news.

Love from your friend,
Auntie May

PART III

AN EVENTFUL YEAR

Reply to yours
Oct 1st. St. Therese of Lisieux

Dear William,

It's clearly all happening in your new world! If I start by summing up what you have told me so far, I can then get to grips with the various aspects.

First let me say, I'm glad you are settled and learning new techniques with Uncle Jack and his assistant – things which you feel will later come in useful at home. I love the idea of signing with a maker's mark, by the way.

So it turns out that Jack and Elisabeth's son, Paul, whom you met last time in Montreal, is on a visit home to discuss if he should try to become a priest. Oh my! Well, that's what you gathered, but he and his mother sometimes speak French together and then you assume they want to be on their own.

I should tell you we call this 'trying his vocation to the priesthood'. 'Vocation' because it is God who calls. He calls us into the world, and calls us to the way of life he in his great love has chosen for us.

We have to find out through prayer what our calling is.

Do you think that Paul's plans have at last nudged his father into finally becoming a Catholic? From what you say I gather he has remained outside the Church all this time. And what's more he turns out to have been your godfather at that long-ago Christening!

Of course! He's your mother's brother and did not share your father's hesitations.

Paul is a little younger than you, isn't he? I suppose his father must have emigrated very soon after your Christening, and married very soon after that.

You add that Jack has taken you with him to the group he now attends at the nearest Catholic church. Or is it two groups? It seems one of these is for people who are interested in coming into the Church, while the other is engaged in worship you always thought of as 'Pentecostal' and there are people there who are Protestant! Please get back to me and explain.

Got to stop there. No, it's not Cuthbert this time. Since the September term started I've been helping at the village school with the children's reading. Two afternoons a week.

God bless you, William!

Love from Rachel May

(Sounds better than 'Auntie' all the time, don't you think?)
From Rachel May Field. (rmayfield96@_____)

Oct 2nd. Guardian Angels 7.00 am

Dear William,

Wow! It didn't sink in that we could exchange emails so quickly. I opened up today and found your reply already in my box.

I'll be back with some answers as soon as I've had time to think. R.M.

From Rachel May Field. (rmayfield96@_____)

Your two groups.
Oct 2nd. Guardian Angels 7.00 pm

Well, well, well! So you are attending RCIA with Jack. It stands for Rite of Christian Initiation of Adults. What a mouthful! The teaching and discussions are to familiarise you with the Catholic Faith but, as I'm sure you realise, you don't have to commit immediately to becoming a Catholic. You should also understand that those Catholics who come to the group are not there just to share with the newcomers but also to refresh their own knowledge and to LEARN. We are always learning. Haven't I said to you so many times 'Life is a journey'?

I remember telling you quite soon after you first got in touch with me, that I felt too many Catholics were living their adult lives on the strength of what they learned as children. Well, that's not quite it, is it? What they learned as children was good; and they have the Liturgy and the Sacraments, and that's a great deal. But each one has his or her own journey and it is right to share, discuss and ask questions along the way. We do not travel alone.

Maybe you and your uncle share as well? After all, he's your longlost godfather, isn't he?

That's it for the moment. I've a whole lot to say though on the subject of the second group you have been introduced to.

Love, Rachel May.
From Rachel May Field. (rmayfield96@_____)

Your Second Group Meeting
Oct.7th. Our Lady of the Rosary

Sorry for the delay, William. I've had a streaming cold. I probably caught it at the school.

Well now, about the second group. Did you assume I would be a stranger to such a session, involving Praise & Worship, followed by Prophecy and Healing? If so, you were wrong. I had regular personal experience of such things before I moved here. And I went to a National Conference for several summers. It was called New Dawn, and its founder had been told by God to hold it at Walsingham in Norfolk, East Anglia. I am going to have to write at length about all this. I'll send each section as an attachment, so look out for them, won't you?

R.M.
From Rachel May Field. (rmayfield96@_____)

! See attached
Oct 15th. St. Teresa of Avila

Dear William,
I am thinking again about your involvement in the lively worship of the charismatic group. (Does the group have a name?)

From what you say you enjoy the praise. Wonderful! St. Paul told the Ephesians '*be filled with the Spirit. . . sing psalms and hymns and inspired songs among yourselves, singing and chanting to the Lord in your hearts.*' (Ep 5:19-20). And according to 2 Samuel (6:14-26) King David danced before the Ark of the Lord. (Note that his wife, Michal, disapproved – but God was on David's side!)

Anyway. . .

Please find attached the first of two documents. This one is about what has become known as Charismatic Renewal. I'm still working on another document about Walsingham; and some more about the Rosary as well.

Love from your friend, R.M.

From Rachel May Field. (rmayfield96@_____)

Attachment One (Oct 15th)

CHARISMATIC RENEWAL

Let's start with **SCRIPTURE:**

It's simple. All you have to do is open your Bible and read the Acts of the Apostles to find numerous examples of miracles, healings and prophecy. These were always known in the Church throughout the centuries, especially in the lives of the Saints. During the general change of ideas in Europe in the late 17th to early 19th centuries – known as the 'Enlightenment' or 'Age of Reason' – the focus, even for Christians, was on the mind. To a certain extent that is still the case – with the mind seen as the way to the heart – but in our own day the Holy Spirit has bestowed the special 'charisms' abundantly (Joel 3). These go straight to heart and mind enabling us to discern and do God's will.

The need is great in our day, because our loving God through whom everything exists, has – in the minds of so many people – ceased to exist!

Then **TRADITION**
Even so, care was taken from the earliest centuries not to over-emphasise miracles. Why? Well it may surprise you to learn that there were a good number of groups calling themselves 'Christian' when they were not. Yes, then, just as today. They represented false beliefs that were not Catholic (not Apostolic, that is); the Gnostics claimed their ideas were more advanced

than the teachings of the Church and some performed 'miracles' through powers given by evil forces. Gnostics are still around in various guises.

And please note that when I say 'not Catholic' I mean definitely un-Christian. This was long before Protestantism. If baptised in the name of Father, Son and Holy Spirit, today's Protestants – although outside the Authority of the Church that Jesus gave to Peter and the other Apostles and thus to the Catholic Bishops – are 'Christian'. They must be acknowledged by Catholics as such, even though they disagree with each other and hold that Catholics have it all wrong. That's the hard part! We believe they are missing out on the fullness of the Faith. How sad Jesus must be that we are not ONE as he prayed to the Father we might be!

But right now let's focus on what the Holy Spirit has been bringing about in our own century.

Again Scripture (see Mark 16:14-20).

Look then at Jesus's own miracles, followed by his words in John 14:12; and in John 15:7-8. He promised that, in the power and grace of the Holy Spirit, his followers would be able to perform miracles as he had done. In a way they already knew, from when he sent out the seventy-two disciples. Yet, miracles – or 'signs' as John calls them – are not an end in themselves. When the seventy-two returned, Jesus said (Lk 10: 20) *'do not rejoice that the spirits submit to you . . . but that your names are written in heaven'*.

Mark, in the final verse of his Gospel, also refers to 'signs' that the Lord sent to confirm the Apostles' preaching (Mk 16:20). Healing, yes! And groups such as yours will offer prayer and laying on of hands, sometimes with an anointing using 'oil of gladness' which is olive oil blessed by the priest for that purpose.

But please note: Tradition (based on James 5:14) gives us also a SACRAMENT: **The Sacrament of the Sick**, to be administered only by the priest, using the oil of chrism, blessed in a special way by the Bishop in Holy Week and used also for the Sacraments of Baptism and Confirmation. You should expect to hear that at the RCIA meeting.

Then there is Prophecy: a huge and most important topic. St. Paul has much to say.

(And so have I!! This is where I became more personally involved.)

I'll have to send a separate letter about the prophetic gifts in the 20th century.

Your friend R.M.

Oct 19th.

St Isaac Jogues and St Jean de Brebeuf

! My studies

Dear William,

Your aunt probably knows more than I do about the Saints who are celebrated on this day. They were French and were martyred in the early 17th Century, on North American soil!

Where was I? Oh yes! Please find attached some further paragraphs, this time on the subject of prophecy.

But meanwhile you have been prompted to ask about the 'studies' I mentioned in my very first letter! In fact, I gather not only Uncle Jack but also Sister Marie, who is partly responsible for the RCIA Group, have both been asking about the basis of what I write to you on the subject of the Faith. What have you been telling them, I wonder?

Well, you can now let them know I took the Diploma Course offered by Our Lady's Catechists. OLC is run under the auspices of the CWL (Catholic Women's League), itself part of WUCWO (World Union of Catholic Women's Organisations). My qualification is a Diploma in Christian Education.

But I am not supposed to be teaching you, William! With you I'm simply sharing what all Catholics are entitled to share: their experience of the Faith and their love of God and his Church.

Now I'll leave you to the attachment. Love, R.M.

From Rachel May Field. (rmayfield96@_____)
ATTACHMENT (2). Prophecy
(Oct 19th.)

Prophecy is something that has always been a major part of
God's revelation of himself to humanity. We say in the Nicene
Creed (the Creed most recited at Mass) that we believe in the
Holy Spirit '....*who has spoken through the prophets*'.

SCRIPTURE
It is God's own Word that speaks through the mouth of the
prophet. [see Isaiah 55: 6-11]. Jesus promised that the Holy Spirit
would '*lead (us) into all truth*' and would sometimes tell of things
to come. (John 14:26; 15:26; 16:13-15.)

I can't resist telling you that I love the passage found in
Numbers 22 to 24. The Israelites were threatening the Moabites.
Balaam was asked, by the Moabite king, to curse Israel, but the
Holy Spirit would not let him and he could only bless! He could
also see from afar one who was to come; King David or even –
further on in time – Our Lord.

What a lot of people do not realise is that in the Church there
are still those called to prophesy. To certain people – perhaps
best known among them the saintly priest Padre Pio – God gives
messages similar to those of the Old Testament prophets. They
are to incite us to change and to warn of where sinfulness leads.
Also in the context of Charismatic Renewal, the Holy Spirit will
guide and uplift some with words they may be asked to pass
on.

The way I think of it is this:
'a word of truth', (in words or sometimes as a 'picture') is given
by the Holy Spirit to a disciple, on a particular occasion, *'to be
used for the general good.'* (I Cor 12:7).

In the Charismatic Renewal, those who are given a 'word' or
'picture' are most often asked to submit it in writing to be
'discerned' by the leaders. Then it will be given out to the group.
This is a safeguard, because St. Paul warned that Satan can
appear as an angel of light (2 Cor 11:14) and some people can
be used as his mouthpiece, or can speak merely as their own
spirits/minds dictate. If the person is known to the group,
however, they may be invited to speak out what they believe the
Lord has given them to say.

Note: sometimes prophecy can come as a 'word of wisdom' or
as a 'word of knowledge'. It gives the person receiving it an
insight and may come with a directive to give a message to
another person, but that is not always to be spoken immediately,
if at all. Such an insight can come frequently to someone who is
'ministering' in prayer for Healing (Prayer Ministry). What they
hear can assist their prayer, and sometimes be spoken to the
person being prayed for, but one must only do this if the Holy
Spirit prompts.

Further to my last

Oct 28th. SS. Simon and Jude, Apostles

Dear William,

I am thinking again about your involvement in the lively worship of the charismatic group. Does the group have a name? You enjoy the PRAISE. Wonderful! We should spend more time praising God.

You particularly commented on the fact that it is a group where Protestants and Catholics come together. Well, Praise the Lord! God knows his purposes, and. . .we have to be honest here. . . the Protestants were the first in the 20th Century to receive this fresh outpouring of the Holy Spirit! That happened at Azusa Street in Los Angeles in 1906. Only much later, in 1968, did some Catholics at Duquesne University decide to take very seriously the Novena between Ascension and Pentecost. The result? Another Pentecost with all its manifestations, including praying in tongues. Presumably they do that at your group?

It is also known that only a few years ago the Lord gave a further blessing in Toronto, now known as 'The Toronto Blessing'. I have not experienced it. Maybe it's your turn to tell me?!

Now.. . .about you (and me). I am sure the Lord has led you to where you are. You are getting so much input from so many sources that there is no need for me to be 'educating' you at this stage. You know I am there for you, praying for you, and ready to answer questions any time.

Please, I'd like to hear about your news – about your work, and what's happening at home in England. Do you hear from your father? Are you in touch with 'the dear girl'? How is Gran?

Who would have thought that we could keep so closely in touch when you are so far away? What a mercy I bothered to set myself up with a computer! I have friends who think themselves too old. Nonsense!

Cuthbert's OK, thank you. Just getting old. It'll have to be much shorter walks this winter.

What's the weather like with you? Autumn must be beautiful. But snow may have fallen by now, I suppose. I think that's it for now. I haven't forgotten that I promised something on Walsingham, and more on the Rosary. I'll focus on those soon.

Goodbye at the end of a busy October!

Love and prayers from your friend, R.M.

From Rachel May Field. (rmayfield96@_____)

! Further to my last
Nov.2nd. All Souls Day

Dear William,

Please find attached my summary on Walsingham and the Rosary.

Meanwhile, I pray daily that you will take this chance of learning all you can from your relatives, and from the Mass you all attend and the groups you and your Uncle go to. I have to say that I am deeply thankful you now have Father Tom and Sister Marie who have authority to pass on the teachings of the Church through RCIA. I am only here to pass on my experience of living the Faith, refreshed by my recent studies.

But let me add that, to have been introduced to the charismatic group (name, please!) is truly a blessing. If you find yourself puzzled about the 'mix' of people from different denominations, remember that Christ's prayer is for UNITY. We Catholics have that unity within the Church, but it does not yet embrace all the baptised, does it? The Spirit blows where he wills!

A good idea would be to read John Chapter 4. Jesus gives the living water to all through his Spirit, as Isaiah prophesied and Jesus told the Samaritan woman.

My news. Up to now the weather has been mild and I have been able to get to Mass most days. Otherwise I am enjoying being here in my cottage, helping at the school and – now the garden is cleared – relaxing with my aged dog by the fire.

Please Note:

I'm more than happy to respond to what you are telling me and add a little here and there to what you are learning. Not on the subject of woodworking, naturally, though I daily thank God for giving you that gift. But still there are some things I'd like to air with you about life as a whole, if you don't mind. And, after all – convenient as emails are – a letter would surely be something more special for Christmas? So I'm planning to post an airmail letter very soon, in time for Christmas (I hope). In fact I must get down to it at once or it'll be too late.
Love, R.M.
From Rachel May Field. (rmayfield96@_____)

ATTACHMENT THREE
(Nov.2nd.)

Well, William, here is what I promised – first, about Walsingham. Walsingham is a small village in Norfolk where the Blessed Virgin Mary appeared to a woman named Richeldis in the year 1062. She asked Richeldis to build a replica of the Holy House of Nazareth where the Angel Gabriel came to her, Mary, at the Annunciation of the Lord. Mary said she wanted people to 'share in her joy'.

Walsingham was a place of pilgrimage for centuries – I think the earliest and one of the greatest shrines in Europe. That all came to an end, of course, with Henry VIII and the so-called

Dissolution of the Monasteries, although Henry had earlier been a pilgrim in Walsingham himself.

Pilgrimages to Walsingham only restarted in our own century. (Sadly, there are separate shrines for Anglicans and Catholics.)

The Rosary is, of course, very much part of any visit to a shrine of Our Lady.

I believe it was St. Dominic who was asked by her to promote this DEVOTION (see next paragraph); and I have already detailed for you the Mysteries of our Lord – Joyful, Sorrowful, and Glorious – which we ponder as we recite the Our Father, Hail Mary and Glory be.

As always, the Mother of Jesus is pointing to her Son and saying, in effect, what she said at the wedding of Cana: '*Do whatever he tells you.*' (Jn 2:5; see also Gen 41:55)

All the apparitions of Our Lady in more recent centuries include her command to be faithful in saying the Rosary.

'Devotions' are what we call particular prayers of the Church that can be used at any time – at home as well as in church. We also speak of someone's 'having a (great) devotion to. . .' let's say the Sacred Heart of Jesus, or Our Lady of Fatima (where she appeared in 1917), or to a particular Saint (as with myself and St. Joseph, remember?)

Sick people can find comfort in simply holding a rosary in their hand. I once went to visit Sister Madeleine when she was seriously ill in hospital. Her hand lay on top of the white bed-cover and she was holding her rosary.

'Hello, Sister,' I said. 'Are you saying the Rosary?'

The hand waved the beads as she replied, 'No, I'm just going like this, and the Lord's doing the rest.'

Prayer itself is listening to God as well as speaking to him – as I'm sure you are well aware by now. St. Teresa of Avila claimed that God heard her slightest whisper. Jesus told us our heavenly Father knows our needs (Mt 6:32). He also said, *'If you ask me anything in my name, I will do it.'* (Jn 14:14).

Yes, prayer can be spontaneous, from the heart. But PRAYER is a habit, William. To have, so to speak, at one's fingertips (which the Rosary literally is) certain prayers of the Saints and of the Church is a great blessing. There are many well-known prayers that we can, so to speak, 'make our own'.

I'll look out for a book of such prayers to send you at home. Meanwhile I feel sure you understand by now the importance of carrying on speaking to the Lord in your heart and listening to his replies.

Nov.9th
Dedication of the Lateran Basilica (Feast)
Dear William,

Your latest email certainly requires some answers.

I am so surprised that you are coming back to England in January. Everyone at home will be delighted to see you!

Then there's your query about Purgatory . . . But you can utterly rely on the Catechism I sent you before you left. Do you have it with you? Does the RCIA group not refer you to it?

Here is one paragraph:

1030 All who die in God's grace and friendship, but still imperfectly purified, are indeed assured of eternal salvation; but after death they undergo purification, so as to achieve the holiness necessary to enter the joy of heaven.

Yes, I do recall writing to you what seems a long time ago about the Church Triumphant and the Pilgrim Church. We were discussing at the time the Church's teaching on the Saints in heaven and those called 'saints' on earth. I confess I left out Purgatory. Those in Purgatory are also known as the 'Suffering Church'. Why 'suffering'? This is not the suffering of the damned in Hell (see CCC 1033), which is permanent and terrible. But, yes, if you study the footnotes in the Catechism (1030 - 32) you'll find the Church does speak of Purgatory as a purifying fire, based on certain passages of Scripture and the formulations of the Councils of Florence and Trent. But, you see, when death overtakes a good person who is ultimately going to heaven, that person may still have sins to expiate.

A priest I know always says that anyone knocked down by a bus after coming out of the confessional will go straight to heaven!! If that is the case, why are we not all lining up to go to Confession?? I also think we are unkind with our expression 'being knocked down by a bus'. Pedestrians should look where they are going!

ABOUT SIN AND ITS EFFECTS
It always seems to me that the most difficult area to deal with in ourselves is *lack of forgiveness*. Forgiving others is hard enough and begins with an act of the will – as I wrote to you when you were having trouble with the master at your prep school. Forgiving yourself is sometimes harder, because you realise that, not only is it your own fault, but the hurt you have caused another person is not automatically wiped out by an apology. Here are two instances:

1) A gives B a black eye. A apologises and B accepts. The black eye does not instantly disappear!

2) You burst open a feather pillow. It is impossible to gather all the feathers up and put them back in. This example illustrates the disastrous effect of gossip and giving away secrets.

We must let grace do its work and make us HOLY. Then we can become Saints and go straight to heaven! Right? We must look to prayer and the Sacraments, and lead a good, kind and humble life! (Micah 6:8)

I must stop there because, as I said, my Christmas letter needs to be in the post by tomorrow if it's to have any chance of reaching you in time.

Love from R.M.
From Rachel May Field. (rmayfield96@_____)

CHRISTMAS LETTER

Dear William,

HAPPY CHRISTMAS! May it be especially blessed as you spend time with your family. I am praying that when you go to Mass, all of you together, you will be drawn to imagine future Christmas Masses where you can participate fully as a Catholic yourself. Such blessings that would bring!

I've been very happy exchanging letters with you and hope we can keep in touch when you are home. I shall always care about what happens to you. And now I'd like to say something about life in general— things that I have learned by experience.

When we started writing, I pointed you to the First Letter of John. We have a loving God. He is the source of all love.

God also knows everything. He knows my heart and he knows yours. He knows his plans for us and for all whom we love. We cannot plan our own lives beyond a certain point and we certainly cannot decide what is right for others. That is why we pray, for ourselves and for those we love, that we will all be shown the right path.

It will be wonderful if your cousin, Paul, truly has a Vocation to the priesthood. Not an easy path, but a privileged one, certainly. Within the Church you otherwise have a choice of living as a single person in the world, or Marriage and Family, or Religious Life (as a missionary, a monk, or even a hermit); a single man may become a Permanent Deacon which is also a special Vocation, and he must then remain single; a married man may (later) become a Permanent Deacon. There have been Deacons since the beginning (Acts 6).

Sometimes we think we have a call to a certain way of life but it turns out not to be our way after all. Where a Vocation is concerned, the final decision is always in the hands of others (the Bishop, the Abbot, the Superior).

The important thing for us all is our commitment to the Christian way of life. For this, we need above all to know in our own hearts what John wrote: GOD IS LOVE.

If he allows sadness to come our way, even that is something that will bring us to eternal life beginning here and now, then ultimately more fully in heaven. For now, my dear young friend, be glad that you are loved and are unique!

At Christmas, the new-born Child speaks to us from the Crib, and from the heart of the Holy Family. My prayer is that you may hear his call from there, as you have done before!

HAPPY NEW YEAR! From your 'Auntie May'

Dec. 8th

The Immaculate Conception

Dear William,

That's great news! Praise the Lord! I'm so thankful you found the courage to ask for prayer from those within your group's Prayer Ministry. I am thanking God for his mercy in freeing you from your eczema. Love, R.M.

P.S. As the group turns out not to have a name, why not suggest 'Living Water' (John 4:14)? That might suit Catholics and Protestants alike, don't you think?

From Rachel May Field. (rmayfield96@_____)

Fourth Sunday of Advent

Dear William,

This is to let you know that a friend has invited me to stay with her over Christmas and New Year. And my neighbour has kindly offered to keep an eye on the cottage while I am away.

You see, I am really sorry to tell you that Cuthbert is no longer with us. He died in his sleep on Dec.15th. Dogs are not intended to stay very long, but the loss to us humans is always huge. At least Cuthbert lived to be 13.

As my PC is not the portable kind, you and I will be out of touch until I get home, which may be even after Epiphany. So I do hope you get my Airmail Letter in time for Christmas. I posted it on Nov. 3rd.

Of course, I miss Cuthbert terribly. The house seems so empty. But I am looking forward to seeing my friend who lives on the south coast of Devon. I'm going by train which is relatively straightforward from here. It will be a treat in lots of ways and we shall go to Mass together.

Looking forward to being in touch with you again. I may even write a letter from there to your home address, to await arrival.

God bless! Love, Auntie May.
From Rachel May Field. (rmayfield96@_____)

LETTER FROM DEVON

Dec.29th Saint Thomas Becket, martyr.
(Patron of the English pastoral clergy)

Dear William,

Here's hoping you've had a wonderful Christmas and New Year, and a safe journey home.

I can't wait to hear all your news but that will only be after I get home to my PC.

I must say, I do love our new way of keeping in touch! In fact I've got so used to it that I've had to ask my friend for pen, paper and an envelope to write this. I didn't bring any of that with me, and the shops are still closed. But at least I found some stamps in my purse.

I am still missing Cuthbert a lot and have to keep reminding myself that if he were still with me I should be alone at home instead of here with Mary. We were together at school, and have always kept in touch, but have not met for a number of years. It's been great catching up.

None of this is what I sat down to write to you about. I want you to know that I am praying for your future. I hope to hear how you are going to be fixed regarding work and whether you will be living at home, with or without your father.

He is also in my prayers. I have always felt that his attitude to God and religion came from his own father. It was fashionable in that generation to claim to be an atheist or agnostic – someone who 'sits on the fence' I always think. It makes me even more thankful that you are looking to find the right path to God and so to Heaven. Pray for your father, William. Prayer achieves so much – and keeps us in a right relationship of dependence on our great God whose love is truly without end.

If you are planning to follow up on what you discovered at the RCIA group while you were away, then the best thing you can do is to read the Catechism and concentrate on the leads it gives into the Scriptures, especially the New Testament (at this stage). Why 'at this stage'? Well, because I'm hoping you are about to enter the fullness of being 'a true and active Christian' as you said in your very first letter you wished to be!

Apart from that, make sure you know and understand the Catholic 'statement of belief' which is the CREED. It is all explained and backed up in the Catechism, naturally, but learning it by heart will enable you to recite it at any time. This would not just be so you can join in at Mass – which I'm sad to say a lot of Catholics don't do very well – but so that you can ponder it in your prayer time.

Thanksgiving is the keynote of private prayer, because it puts us in a right relationship with our God. However hard life becomes, try to find one particular reason each day for thanking him. After my first husband died, I remember on one particular day thanking God for a new, blue umbrella!

As soon as I've settled back into Field Cottage, I'll get on to my PC and see if you have emailed me any news. I'd like to hear your plans, and please do not hesitate to ask me anything you feel I might have an answer to.

Finally, thank you for trusting me during these years with such important questions, and your own thoughts. It has been a privilege. Thank you, too, for my bookcase. Do you think if you made more they would sell well?

I've had a lovely time here with Mary but, as the old song says, 'there's no place like home' I rather think you may be glad of your home, too.

Love, Rachel May.

Jan 17th,

St. Anthony, Abbot

Dear William,

Such a lot of news from you! I'll get back to you on all of it but first I want to let you know my plans because it may mean being out of touch for a while.

When Cuthbert was still with me, I decided to soldier on with my arthritis, but my GP has now referred me for a hip replacement. Realising I shan't be allowed to do the garden for several months, and that driving will be a problem, has made me think I should start planning a move into town. Field Cottage will have to go up for sale and I shall be looking for an apartment.

Yes, it's 'all change' round here! So, as you can see, William, this is not a good time for me to be buying tickets to come and see you! Firstly, I have no idea when my hospital place will come up, and after the operation I shall be staying a couple of weeks with some Sisters of Mercy who take guests. Secondly, no one ever knows how long a house will take to sell, or whether the right apartment will come up when I need it. It's impossible to make any other plans. So sorry! Later on, maybe?

Now! Your news. . . Yes, it's a wonderful idea to approach Fr. Declan at Sacred Heart and ask if you can 'take instruction' and 'be received' at the Easter Vigil. I think suggesting Alicia as your 'sponsor' should do the trick, because she and Gran are such devout members of his congregation. You did tell me before that

Alicia often goes to Mass in the week, morning or evening, depending on how she can manage her hours at work.

Clearly you and she are in touch, and it's nice to hear you have been round to Gran's place a few times –having a meal and joining in with the Rosary after.

No, I'm not surprised Alicia refuses to come round to your house! Can't you just invite her to visit the workshop and join you in the garden?

Again no, I don't for a minute imagine it's just that she is so fully committed to work and to her Gran! Probably it's hard for you to realise how she has been brought up? Truth is, that while a large percentage of young people think nothing of spending time alone in each other's places that is not compatible with a true Christian lifestyle. Too much temptation. Please, don't get offended! Martin and Richard's family would also agree, surely? And you – who hung out with their crowd at college, and have now been studying the Scriptures and the Catechism – should be happy to honour Alicia's wishes and keep to her standards. Such a spiritual young lady! Gossip, however ill-founded, can do such damage and cause such pain, believe me!

On the question of the house itself, it's splendid that you have sole use of it for the time being and can keep your workshop and make some of your living from that. I've been thinking about the garden, too. Is it very big? I gather your father's living permanently in London now. Did he arrange for someone to come and clear the garden in the autumn when the house was empty?

It's clear you will have your work cut out, what with your efforts to build up a business, and whatever supply teaching you can get to provide a fuller income meanwhile. And then spending time in the garden, at Church, and out with Alicia!

That I'll be praying for you goes without saying. I'm imploring God already for a 'yes' from Fr Declan. Maybe you hadn't got round to thinking about the date of the Easter Vigil, but it actually falls on April 3rd this year! Your birthday! Do please let me know at once whether you get the go-ahead. Could you dare to suggest he might test you on your knowledge? I'm sure you'd pass.

I'll be turning on my PC every few minutes to see if you've sent a message. I can't remember if I told you, but I decided to manage without a landline here, thinking to be up to date with a mobile; but the signal is unreliable – except when you stand halfway down the garden! And it's hard to manage the umbrella at the same time, I can tell you. Always raining here!

Well, that's all our news dealt with. I promise not to write such long emails in future, but it looks as if it will be important to keep in touch. News will be buzzing back and forth for a while, I'm certain!

God bless! Love, Rachel May.
From Rachel May Field. (rmayfield96@_____)

Praise the Lord
Jan 20th

William dear, that's such good news! Is your uncle going to be received this Easter? You say Fr Declan hasn't promised that yet for you, but he is going to see you once a week himself and will let you know. I suppose all you have to do now is swallow the Catechism whole?

With prayers for you all, Love, R.M.
From Rachel May Field. (rmayfield96@_____)

! Attachment

email Jan 25th

Ah! So Fr Declan was not so keen on your description of charismatic renewal. Sorry. I should have thought to warn you. You have to be aware there were already great changes in the Church after the Second Vatican Council and older priests (not to mention older parishioners!) had first to get used to Mass in their own language, and to the priests celebrating facing the congregation. The new emphasis was on lay people taking a more obvious part. I mean not just 'hearing' Mass in Latin.

We are quite far down the line now but there's also the 'new' teaching that we must do more to recognise 'other Christians' – on account of their baptism as I've said – and yet we must still fit this in with our belief in the One, Holy, Catholic and Apostolic Church as the true way.

We who love the Renewal have to recognise that the praise and worship which means so much to us and makes our faith come alive, can come over to our fellow-Catholics as – what shall I say? –'not what we Catholics do' ? It seems like one thing too many to some people. I've more than once got the reaction: 'We don't want all that happy-clappy here!'

You will have already worked out that it would be best to tone down your enthusiasm and follow Fr Declan's lead. He will be testing and completing your knowledge along the lines of the Catechism. Leave the task of creating understanding to the Holy

Spirit, William! Our Pope is with us and the message will get through. I trust my attachment will encourage you. Fr Declan will also be aware that you need to be firm in your faith as you will encounter opposition. More on that in my next. Stick like glue to the Catechism and the Creed, and your prayers.

It's good you've put your name down for supply teaching. Maybe you'll be back teaching 8-yr-olds soon? God knows!

Meanwhile, ask St. Joseph to watch over your efforts to make a place for yourself in your trade and build up some interest.

Small items to begin with? Maybe Alicia will show her friends the jewellery box you made for her and that will bring some custom?

Please note that ATTACHMENT (4) is quoted from one of my essays and refers to two documents concerning lay people in the Church: I'm talking about the present Pope's Apostolic Exhortation known as **Christifidelis Laici**, itself based on the Vatican II document known as **Apostolicam actuositatem**.

Latin titles are given to such documents, using the opening words of each. This is in keeping with the universality (catholicity) of the Church. The documents are all in Latin to start with and then translation into English and other languages comes soon after.

Yes, the cottage is on sale. I'll have to be patient on that score,

and about waiting for the operation. It's all in the Lord's hands
–as are you! Love, R.M.

From Rachel May Field. (rmayfield96@_____)

ATTACHMENT (4)
Tradition, too, has its modern message, as proclaimed by
Vatican II (AA 33) and reiterated by Pope John Paul in
Christifidelis Laici 2:

> *'The council, then, makes an earnest plea in the Lord's name that
> all people give a glad, generous and prompt response to the
> impulse of the Holy Spirit and to the voice of Christ, who is
> giving them an especially urgent invitation at this moment.'*

Jan 27th.
Dear William,

So it's decided! You will be coming into the Church at the Easter
Vigil. Thank God!

It's been quite a journey. I'm really rejoicing!

Yet now's the time for me to sound a note of warning. . . It's not
for nothing that Easter is preceded by Lent, with its stress on
prayer and fasting. Nor that we are asked to follow Jesus'
example and spend time in the wilderness. You know well – but
need to be especially aware at this time – that we have an enemy.
Satan, the Devil, whom Jesus called '*the prince/ruler of this world*'
(John 14:30) tempts us directly and also through 'the world' and
'the flesh'. He used Scripture to tempt the Son of God, after
Jesus' Baptism and before he began preaching the Kingdom.

I've said before that I'm not the gambling sort, but it wouldn't
surprise me if various obstacles, large and small, appear in your
path. Faith must be tested. (I Peter 5:8-9; Ephesians 4:26-27).

If Alicia has a book with the Morning, Evening and Night Prayer
of the Divine Office in it – which wouldn't at all surprise me –
then ask her to show you the Scripture Readings for Night
Prayer. They include the two I've just referred to, and others that
speak of total reliance on God. Walk minute by minute with your
guardian angel!

I've asked Fr John here to offer a Mass for you on February 2nd. Such a special day!

God bless! Keep in touch when you can.

My prayers are with you. Love, R.M.

Feb 2nd.
Solemnity of the Presentation of the Lord (Candlemas)

Dear William,

Please don't get disheartened. The dear Lord is hurt by our lack
of trust. You are to be received at Sacred Heart. There must be a
statue in the church somewhere, where you can kneel, and light
a candle, and talk to Jesus like the child who has more than once
felt close to him in the Crib?

If you are still feeling shy of statues – despite being familiar with
those at Gran's place – then why not adopt the prayer that is
frequently on the lips of many a Catholic: 'Sacred Heart of Jesus
I put all my trust in you.' If you only understood how close
Jesus is to you, you would be content to live one minute at a
time. He knows your needs.

Love, R.M.
From Rachel May Field. (rmayfield96@_____)

Feb 4th.
What a mercy

William, you are so fortunate. That is a great kind of statue to
have in your church. Seeing Jesus standing there with his arms
opened wide in welcome always makes me want to rush up to
him for a hug. Love, R.M.

From Rachel May Field. (rmayfield96@_____)

Feb 8th.
Dear William,

Please listen to Alicia. She can help you understand Mary. I
remember writing to you about her a long time ago. Mary can
'hide you under her mantle' and she is 'the New Eve', the 'full
of grace' who treads down that old 'serpent', the Devil.

Anyone who has been brought up without knowledge of her
and with a Protestant background, struggles against having
been told that Catholics make too much of her. Her role is given
her by God. She is daughter of the Father, spouse of the Holy
Spirit, and Mother of the Son. She will guard and guide you, as
will the Saints and the Angels.

God bless! R.M.
From Rachel May Field. (rmayfield96@_____)

See of St. Peter the Apostle

Feb. 22nd.

Dear William,

I AM SO SORRY! It was hard to take, but you were right to tell me. I had no idea I sounded as if I wanted to run your life for you! I promise to stand well back while you get everything sorted.

Prayerfully, 'Auntie May'.

P.S. Have a good Lent. I'll let you know if I have important news from here.

From Rachel May Field. (rmayfield96@_____)

Viewing
March 9th. St. Frances of Rome,
(wife, mother and then Religious)

Dear William,

Some people came to look at the house but I think they found it
too small, and I'm not expecting an offer. I'm starting my
Novena to St. Joseph tomorrow, and have ordered the book I
promised you.

Love, 'Auntie May'.

P.S. If you have anything to share, please do. I promise not to
boss you about.
From Rachel May Field. (rmayfield96@_____)

Operation brought forward
March 17th.

Dear William,
I've just had notice that I can get in right away to have my hip done. A cancellation. So now I've to make last minute arrangements, pack my things and let the Sisters know as well. I hope they will have a room for me when I need it.

Of course no emails. This will be your last from me until I get back here. If you write to me at Field Cottage it will reach me eventually.

You are in safe hands. That I shall be praying for you daily goes without saying. (But I've gone and said it! Typical! But you know me by now.)

Love, R.M.
From Rachel May Field. (rmayfield96@_____)

LETTER AT EASTER

Dear William,

Bless you for the lovely card! My friend picked it up from Field Cottage on Thursday and brought it to me. I'm in the cottage hospital. The GP found me a place here until the Sisters can have me. The operation went well but there was some problem with an allergy or something. I have to leave it to the experts. I am out of bed several times a day and getting on all right with my crutches.

Thank you for apologising as well. You are long forgiven, and I hope I am, too. I was so disappointed I couldn't be with you this weekend but you have had your friends at your side.

It's so strange not being in church for the Easter Triduum, but Fr John brought me Communion. Praise God! And Our Lord is with us at all times and in all places.

Love, Auntie May.

LETTER FROM HOME

May 31st.
The Visitation

Dear William,

As there have been no emails from you I thought I'd stick to letters.

I finally got back here at the beginning of the month and can now manage with one crutch only. Soon it will be just my stick, I hope.

The man I had hired to look after the garden has kept it looking nice, and now a young couple are showing interest in the house. They are newly married and he works with the police in another area. I do hope they agree to go ahead and buy.

It's such a task clearing a house, and I'm having to arrange temporary storage because the right apartment has not turned up yet. I am not keeping much actually, but the oak bookshelf will go with me, don't worry! It is a prized possession and will be just right to hold those books I feel I just can't do without.

The neighbours have all been very helpful and we had a 'Garage Sale' for charity. That proved a good idea for getting rid of every-thing I shall no longer need. I've kept a photo of my younger self with my hand on a younger Cuthbert beside me.

I have not yet found the apartment I want, near the church and the shops. They say I should be on the ground floor as there's some concern about my heart. Can't be much wrong, though, when you think of all the exercise I used to get in the garden and on dog-walks.

Before I forget, when this place is cleared I shall be going to stay with Mary, travelling by taxi and train as I did before, but this time with assistance.

Don't try to email, William, as my PC is closed down ready for the move. We can keep in touch by letter. God bless you!

Love, Auntie May.

Letter - Moving!

July 16th.

Our Lady of Mount Carmel

Dear William,

Sorry it's been so long. But the news is good. The house is sold, the young couple are due to move in very soon, and I am settled in my new apartment. It's upstairs, but there is a lift and it does mean I have a good view of the garden. No gardening for me, I'm glad to say. We pay towards the maintenance.

Father John is to retire now and we are getting a new priest in September. I am seriously hoping I shall have a chance to teach catechetics, using my Diploma at last. I should enjoy preparing people for Baptism – that is to say, helping parents to understand the seriousness and the depth of the Sacrament and the path they have chosen for their child.

I will email you the full address of my flat when I get the PC up and running. I could send it you with this letter but a) I'm not sure of the postcode and b) an email might actually reach you sooner!

My best love, your friend
Rachel May

Your letters received

August 3rd.

Feria

Dear William,

I'm back on my PC and your letters have just come through, forwarded from Field Cottage. I'm going to read them properly and answer as soon as I can find a decent length of time.

I am going shopping first, though not for much as the lift is out of order and I've been told not to carry much coming up the stairs. But before I go, here's my new address: 10, Bakers Court. I still haven't checked the postcode but I expect you'll be emailing anyway.

Love R.M.

From Rachel May Field. (rmayfield96@_____)

PART IV

WILLIAM TAKES UP
THE STORY

WILLIAM TAKES UP
THE STORY

I WILL NEVER KNOW HOW MUCH AUNTIE MAY READ OF the letters she had from me that day, now so many years ago. But it's not a day I ever forget. She had fallen, poor lady, as she made her way up the stairs. That day, August 3rd, was the day she died. They blamed her heart.

I had sent several emails but had no reply. In the end her executors got in touch with me. By that time, Fr John had seen to the Requiem Mass and burial, but I have since had many Masses offered for the repose of her soul. It was she who taught me the importance of that. My cousin Paul, who was by then on his way to becoming 'Father Paul' also promised to have a Mass offered at the famous Oratory of St. Joseph in Montreal. Auntie May would have loved that place. She had such a devotion to St. Joseph!

My dear friend had left me all her Catholic books and the bookcase I had made and, tucked between the books, I found the photo of her with Cuthbert. Amazing to think the three of us never met!

Now... I suppose I'd better start by filling you in from right back then! Here's a summary of what had been going on with me from Lent until July that year:

The first of those 'testings' May had warned me about came in

March when I went to my mother's grave at St. Mary's. The Vicar saw me and questioned me about the news that I was becoming Catholic. He maintained my mother had clearly meant me to be Church of England. Really? And then he asked, was it all because of 'that girl'? I felt mad at first but God helped me and I forgave.

The next thing was Gran got ill and so only dear Alicia was with me at the Easter Vigil, my 23rd birthday and the start of my new life in the Church.

We spent a lot of time with Gran that week, and one time she asked to speak to me alone. She knew Alicia well and she knew God's ways. I wish I had listened.

Gran got worse and was moved to hospital, and sadly died a few days later. The Requiem was at Sacred Heart and Alicia's parents stayed at my place that time.

Another tricky situation was that Dad had wanted to come at Easter with his lady friend. I had to put him off with the news that I was going to be received into the Catholic Church and Auntie May might be coming. I thought he, too, would be mad at me but actually he wasn't. He had got it into his head I was doing it to please Alicia!

I don't have the letters I wrote to May but it's likely I told her the garden was coming on; my name was down for supply teaching; and I was beavering away in the workshop.

I should say right away that bespoke furniture needs rich customers. The business didn't take off for a long while but when it did it was partly down to Uncle Jack's having taught me the value of that maker's mark, a special signature carved on each piece. And Dad also did his bit whipping up custom among his contacts!

I'm sure I'd told her I'd had six weeks' supply teaching at the Sacred Heart Primary before the summer term ended, taking the class of a teacher who took early maternity leave.

Some of the teachers and parents I met seemed almost to resent my enthusiasm for the Catholic Faith! It was a bit of an eye-opener after Auntie May's strict teaching, but I persevered in prayer, and the kids were great. To be honest a lot of the Catholic adults I've met over the years do not seem to me to value the Faith as they should. Wasn't that just what dear May had hinted at?

Let me see. . . In June Dad turned up, trying to play the man, but clearly devastated. He'd had some idea of marrying in a registry office, but then found out the woman was carrying on with someone else!! He went straight back to London, changed the locks and went on a business trip to the US. After that he was with me at weekends and put in some hard work on the garden. God bless him!

Then there was Alicia. . .

She was renting Gran's house, working hard, but planning to go back to her family soon; to get a job there, I was thinking. Frankly, Gran's words had slipped my mind, and at that time I hadn't yet recalled something else – something Auntie May had written when she first heard of 'the dear girl'. That came after.

I had told Auntie May I felt Alicia and I were in love. To be fair, I think Alicia thought so, too. But Gran had seen beyond that - and so had Auntie May, even though she hadn't even met her. Then, one summer evening as we were sitting in the garden, on the special seat I had made for us, Alicia decided to share that she felt God was calling her to belong to him alone. In other words, she was planning to 'try her Vocation' as a Religious Sister!

Why hadn't I seen it coming? I suppose my love for her had not let me see beyond her involvement with work at the shop, and her warm friendship with all she met. I can see now that my memory of her as a bridesmaid, and my hopes of her as my bride-to-be had blinded me to her deep spirituality and the direction in which our loving God was leading her. But she was right, and she has since been warmly welcomed into a community of Poor Clare Sisters. How blessed they are!

All this I had relayed to 'Auntie May' and I am sure that she is praying for each of us in heaven.

At New Year, those of us still on earth left the old millennium behind. The world moved on. . and so did I.

Before my next birthday I finally passed my driving test and, whenever I could get away, used to go on pilgrimage to the Shrine of Our Lady at Walsingham. Such a holy place!

God is always with us but where Mother Mary invites us to draw near, she also invites us to share her firm belief in the promises of her Son! I still felt drawn to the path of Marriage and Family and once I was given a 'word of knowledge' there in the words of Matthew 6:33.

God works in mysterious ways!

It was at Walsingham that I eventually met Deborah, who has been my wife for some years now. As a child, she had come to England from Uganda. We have two children. Our eldest is Michael Joseph (Deborah's orphaned nephew whom we adopted four years after we married.) He is now 8 years old. His little sister was born to us three years later. Her name is Mary Clare.

TIME TO CONCLUDE

A UNTIE MAY HELPED ME SO MUCH WITH HER TEACHINGS. As I said at the beginning, this book has been my way of sharing with you everything that good friend wrote to me about belonging to the One, Holy, Catholic and Apostolic Church. Yet I now understand it was all along the path chosen by God, our loving Father, who has continually enriched my life with his grace. He has blessed me in good times and bad, making me grow in my love for Jesus: while guiding and prompting me through his Holy Spirit.

All this had been given to me at my baptism but I needed to acknowledge it and grow in the gift of eternal life – which is ours now, and for ever in heaven.

'Life is a journey.' (Recognise those words?) Since coming into the Church I have gained so much. Consider:

➢ The grace of the Sacraments, and the teachings of the Church.
➢ As often as I am present at Mass I give thanks that I am a witness to and take part in the sacrifice of Our Lord and Saviour, Jesus Christ, who died for us on the Cross and rose from death on the third day.
➢ The Word of God in the Liturgy, through the Scriptures and in the Body and Blood of Christ which we receive in Holy Communion, as he commanded.

➤ At God's right hand, he pleads for us sinners as we
   walk the pilgrim way.
➤ We have the angels to guard us and the saints to pray
   for us.
➤ We pray for each other here on earth and for the souls
   in Purgatory, especially those who have no-one to pray for
   them.

In our family we pray the Rosary together daily, guided by
Auntie May's instruction. Also on Thursdays we now add in the
MYSTERIES OF LIGHT introduced by Pope John Paul II in 2002.
These set before us Jesus' adult life: his Baptism, the Wedding
at Cana, the Preaching of the Kingdom, the Transfiguration and
finally the Institution of the Eucharist.

My prayer is that by my sharing with you Rachel May's letters
and my story you will have seen something of the LOVE OF
GOD, and the joy and hope of belonging to Christ's Body, the
Church, also known as Christ's Bride as it is through her that he
bestows on us the eternal life he won for us by his Life, Death
and Resurrection.

FUTURE HOPES
My first hope is to make it to heaven!

I love my wife and the children, thank God for them and pray
for them always.

Maybe when they are older I may think about serving the
Church as a Permanent Deacon. Who knows?

Eastertide 2012

ACKNOWLEDGEMENTS

My heartfelt gratitude to all who have supported me in the writing of this book.

Thanks to Jenny for a comfortable home during lockdown where I could write in peace, and to my prayer-partner, Marion, for dozens of phone calls and her many prayers.

Twofold thanks to Sue who, as my tutor on the OLC Diploma Course, always insisted on high standards, and who then undertook to proof-read my manuscript and to comment appreciatively.

Thanks to Adeline, Adrienne and others in Oxford who were encouraging and happy to read samples of a work in progress. Thanks also to my current fellow-parishioners at St. Begh's Church, Whitehaven, for their support and apparent eagerness to have this book, written by me their new catechist.

And, of course, a huge vote of thanks to Toni and Gerard Pomfret of *Goodnews Books* who have supplied me with Christian literature, information and encouragement over many years, and have now undertaken to publish *Letters to William* under the banner of their publishing arm, *New Life Publishing*.

Above all, I thank God for his many gifts and especially for all who have loved and cherished, inspired and taught me, throughout the years. *To him be the glory for ever and ever. Amen.*

Margaret Stevens

BIBLIOGRAPHY

(Publications cited from / referred to, all of which were
available prior to 1999 when the letters themselves ended)

• *The New Jerusalem Bible, Pocket Edition*, (London 1990, Darton, Longman & Todd,)
• *The New Jerusalem Bible, Standard Edition*, (London 1985, Darton Longman & Todd)
• *Catechism of the Catholic Church*, (London 1994, Geoffrey Chapman, a Cassell imprint)
• *VATICAN COUNCIL II,THE CONCILIAR AND POST-CONCILIAR DOCUMENTS*, General Editor: Flannery, Austin, O.P. (1975, United States, Pillar Books, by arrangement with Costello Publishing Company, Inc.) ©1975 Costello Publishing Company, Inc. and Reverend Austin Flannery, O.P.
• *MORNING & EVENING PRAYER*, from The Divine Office, London 1976 ©Harper Collins 1976
• *THE SUNDAY MISSAL, A NEW EDITION*, Texts approved for use in England and Wales, Ireland, Scotland. Collins Liturgical, a Division of Harper Collins Publishers. © Compilation and editorial matters 1975,1976,1977, 1982 and 1984 William Collins Sons & Co Ltd
• *The Didache* to be found in *ANCIENT CHRISTIAN WRITERS VOLUME VI*, Translated by James A. Kliest, S.J., Ph.D.Westminster, Maryland The Newman Press, London. Longman's Green and Co. © 1948 by Rev. Johannes Quasten & Rev. Joseph C. Plumpe. Printed in the USA

Further Reading

The Didache Bible, Ignatius Press, ISBN 9781939231147

The Catechism of the Catholic Church, Catholic Truth Society, ISBN 9781784691066

The Four Witnesses, the Early Church in Her Own Words, Rod Bennett, Ignatius Press, ISBN 9780898708479

The Lambs Supper the Mass as Heaven on Earth, Scott Hahn, Darton, Longman, & Todd, ISBN 9780232525007

The Creed, Ambrose Walsh, New Life Publishing, ISBN 9781912237142

This is My Body, Ian Petit OSB, New Life Publishing, ISBN 9781903623282

Love is The Key, Fr Chris Thomas, New Life Publishing, ISBN 9781903623640

Encountering Jesus, Pat Collins, C.M., New Life Publishing, ISBN 9781903623121

Further copies of this book
can be obtained from
Goodnews Books
Upper level
St. John's Church Complex
296 Sundon Park Road
Luton, Beds. LU3 3AL
www.goodnewsbooks.co.uk
orders@goodnewsbooks.co.uk
+44 (0) 1582 571011